D0772609

CP         は 12⁵⁰

# The Statistical System of Communist China

CHOH-MING LI

# The Statistical System
# of Communist China

UNIVERSITY OF CALIFORNIA PRESS
BERKELEY AND LOS ANGELES, 1962

UNIVERSITY OF CALIFORNIA PRESS
BERKELEY AND LOS ANGELES, CALIFORNIA
CAMBRIDGE UNIVERSITY PRESS
LONDON, ENGLAND
LIBRARY OF CONGRESS CATALOG CARD NUMBER: 62–9725
PRINTED IN THE UNITED STATES OF AMERICA

# Preface

This study is a product of the Research Project on the Agriculture of Communist China, conducted at the Berkeley campus of the University of California. While dealing primarily with the validity of Chinese official statistics from the standpoint of the development of the statistical system, it may be of use to those interested in the planning mechanism of the country. Despite the differences in economic and political systems among the underdeveloped countries today, the problems that China encountered in developing a national statistical system should be illuminating to other countries striving to carry out their development programs.

The study is based entirely on documentary sources published by Peiping. Visiting Hong Kong during the summer of 1961, I was able to interview some one recently fled from the mainland, who since 1957 had been engaged in statistical work in the Industrial and Mining Bureau of a *hsien* (county) in one of the provinces. His description of the statistical service at that administrative level substantiates the findings here, thus allaying much of my anxiety over the possibility that the actual working of the statistical system was not faithfully reflected in the evidences examined. The results of the interview, too late to be included in this volume, will be published separately as an article.

The few translations of Chinese-language sources, officially prepared by the Foreign Language Press of Peiping, have not been used in this study. All direct quotations are my own translations from the original Chinese texts. For phonetic rendering of Chinese names and words, there are several systems in use, including the one introduced by Peiping in recent years. I have not adhered to any particular system, but rather to a usage that I believe to be generally acceptable in this country. To conform to general usage, a few names in this study have a form slightly different from that in my previous publications.

I am indebted to many friends and colleagues who helped in the preparation of this study. Special gratitude is due to Professor Simon Kuznets of Harvard University, experienced in studying statistics of various countries in different stages of economic development, who carefully read through the manuscript. Dr. Esther Morrison of the Center for Chinese Studies and the staff of the Research Project on Agriculture in Berkeley helped in the preparation of the manuscript for the press. The University of California Press, in particular Mr. Philip E. Lilienthal and Dr. Max E. Knight, were singularly helpful in expediting and editing the publication.

Parts of chapters ii and vi were read before one of the panel sessions of the annual meeting of the American Economic Association at St. Louis toward the end of 1960, and have since been published in the Association's *Proceedings* in May, 1961. Similarly, parts of chapters vii and viii have been presented as a paper to the Symposium on Economic and Social Problems of the Far East, sponsored by the University of Hong Kong on the occasion of its Golden Jubilee in September, 1961; the paper will be published in the proceedings of the Symposium.

Berkeley, California

C. M. Li

# Contents

## TABLES

# Abbreviations

| | |
|---|---|
| CCYC | *Ching-chi yen-chiu* [Economic Research] |
| CHCC | *Chi-hua ching-chi* [Planned Economy] |
| CHYTC | *Chi-hua yü t'ung-chi* [Planning and Statistics] |
| HC | *Hung-ch'i* [Red Flag] |
| HH | *Hsüeh-hsi* [Study] |
| HHPYK | *Hsin-hua pan-yueh-k'an* [New China Semi-Monthly] |
| JMJP | *Jen-min jih-pao* [People's Daily] |
| TCKT | *T'ung-chi kung-tso* [Statistical Work] |
| TCKTTH | *T'ung-chi kung-tso t'ung-hsin* [Statistical Bulletin] |
| TCYC | *T'ung-chi yen-chiu* [Statistical Research] |
| TKP | *Ta Kung Pao* [Impartial Daily] |

# CHAPTER I

# Introduction

OBJECTIVES AND BASIS OF THE STUDY

One of the most baffling problems in contemporary Chinese economic studies is the validity of official statistics. The development of research in this field depends on the solution. Since official admission of gross exaggerations in the 1958 statistics, the problem has become even more acute. In the discussion of claims and counterclaims, appeals to common sense are not sufficient. There is need for substantial evidence with which to form a judgment.

This study, dealing with the statistical system of Communist China, will not concern itself with statistical definitions and concepts, nor will it enter into an examination of official statistics. Both of these approaches have been taken elsewhere.[1] Rather, it will attempt to appraise the quality of official statistics through a study of the development and the inner working of the system. This will require a painstaking investigation of a mass of details. To obtain a proper perspective the subject will be introduced by an evaluation of the statistical services before 1949.

The establishment of an effective statistical system has now been recognized as indispensable for an underdeveloped country in its programing of economic development. The

[1] See, for example, my *Economic Development of Communist China*, Berkeley and Los Angeles: University of California Press, 1959, and "Economic Development," *The China Quarterly*, 1: 35–50, January-March, 1960.

system must regularly produce, for publication or otherwise, quantitative information national in scope and reasonably accurate in accordance with its own sets of definitions. Two extreme types of national system may be distinguished: The noncentralized system, in which central and local government agencies, trade bodies, and private institutes periodically collect and publish quantitative data on various activities of the society; the more comprehensive the coverage and the more accurate the data, the better will be the national system; although there is no centralized control of statistical services, the data represented a national whole—it is in this sense that a national statistical system exists in the United States. The system operated by the state statistical agency with a nationwide organization, on the other hand, is responsible for standardization of methods, concepts and schedules, supervision and coördination of the services in business enterprises and government departments, and centralization of control over all national data with regard to their utilization and release. Such a system is apparently vital to a centrally planned and directed economy. The example *par excellence* is that of the Soviet Union.

In many underdeveloped countries today, bcause of the lack of private resources or initiative to collect statistics, a central bureau with a national network of offices is often established, serving as the foundation for the development of a national system that necessitates varying degrees of central participation and control. As a case study, the development of the system in China is particularly instructive in bringing out sharply both the nature of the formidable obstacles that stand in the way in a densely populated country with a huge agricultural sector, and the various organizational and statistical-control measures that have been adopted to overcome them.

A word should be said about the sources of information. Except for the pre-1949 development, this study relies heavily on the information in the official journals of the State Statistical Bureau of Peiping, published since April, 1954. The bureau's journal was first issued as a monthly, under the title *T'ung-chi kung-tso t'ung-hsin* [Statistical Bulletin]. It was changed into a semimonthly in 1956, and renamed *T'ung-chi kung-tso* [Statistical Work] in 1957. In the first nine months of 1958 the State Bureau also published a monthly, *T'ung-chi yen-chiu* [Statistical Research]; after the September issue it was merged into the *Statistical Work*. In January, 1959, the journal combined with *Chi-hu ching-chi* [Planed Economy], the official monthly of the State Planning Commission since January, 1955, to become *Chi-hua yü t'ung-chi* [Planning and Statistics], a semimonthly for the first three months of 1959, and a monthly since then.

Designed primarily for communicational and training purposes within the national statistical and planning services,[2] these journals were not open to public subscription on the mainland until 1956 and were not made generally available until the "free discussion period" in 1957 when current issues were allowed to be exported. Since February, 1959, they have again been withdrawn from public circulation. The search for the missing issues has been a research effort in itself.

DEVELOPMENT OF STATISTICAL SERVICES BEFORE 1949

Before 1949 only a rudimentary statistical system existed in China. It may be traced back to 1931 when directly under the president of the republic the Directorate General of Budgets, Accounts and Statistics was established, where the Bureau of Statistics was in charge of unifying the methods of compiling statistics and of the appointment of statistical personnel

---

[2] For example, an instruction issued by the State Bureau on September 20, 1954, was to the effect that all replies to readers concerning statistical schedules, methods, and regulations, published in the official journal in the name of any one of the bureau's departments or of the journal itself, carried the force of an official directive.

in all government departments. Statistical offices were set up in all central government ministries and in provincial governments. Up to 1949 this organization rarely reached the *hsien* level, but the *hsien* magistrates were expected to produce such statistical data from time to time as the central and provincial authorities required. Moreover, the offices that had been established were not able to develop their work as expected, and the network represented more an expansion of bureaucracy than an enlargement of services. This is attested by the fact that in spite of repeated orders from the president, the bureau was not able to produce a single issue of a statistical yearbook until 1948, and this turned out to be not much of an improvement over the four issues of statistical abstracts published previously.

The reasons for this arrested development are not far to seek. First, statistical information was considered as part of political intelligence which should not fall into the hands of dissenters. When the national government was first established in Nanking in 1927, the president of the Legislative Yuan set up a relatively effective department of statistics to gather information for law-enacting purposes. The data so gathered soon proved to be embarrasing to the groups contending for power. As a result, the function of collecting statistics was shifted to and centralized in the Bureau of Statistics in 1931 under the direct control of the president of the republic. This identification of statistics with political intelligence had the effect of discouraging not only trained statisticians from joining the service but those who had joined from taking any initiative to undertake pioneering work. It is significant that the secret police organizations of the Kuomintang and of the Military Affairs Commission had both operated under the name of statistical bureaus. The only important innovation in statistical services during the Nationalist period was the compilation of index numbers of prices, cost of living, and wages in a few cities—subjects of no political significance at the time. Several university institutes and private organizations also undertook various field surveys with the permission and coöperation of government agencies, but they were mostly local in nature.

The second and equally important reason is that statistics were not relied upon for policy-making, because the statistical information then available, was neither up-to-date nor accurate. But if policy makers had been conscious of the need, the statistical service would have been improved. Actually there was no real appreciation of the importance of statistics, which are a modern tool in social accounting. Appreciation must be derived from an understanding of the value of scientific analysis. Such understanding was lacking both among government authorities and the general public. Decisions were made on the basis of intuition and common sense without the aid of factual data. Even as late as 1948 when the first statistical yearbook was published, the director-general wrote of the development of statistical services in the following terms: "[Since 1931], although there have been some acomplishments in the organization of offices, the formulation of procedures, and the collection and publication of materials, the practical application of statistics awaits further effort." [3]

Under these circumstances, the collection of statistical data by central government agencies and provincial governments was perfunctory. There was no demand, and indeed no need, for accuracy and adequate coverage. This is not to say that none of the pre-1949 official statistics were of any value. The trade returns of the customs—and to a lesser extent, the reports of the post offices—stood out as the best of all official statistics with a quality comparable to that of the West, although the credit for this accomplishment should go to the

[3] Directorate General of Budgets, Accounts and Statistics, Bureau of Statistics, *Chung-hua-min-kuo t'ung-chi nien-chien* [Statistical Yearbook of the Republic of China], Nanking: 1948, preface.

early foreign administration of these services. Among other government agencies, the National Agricultural Research Bureau, the Ministry of Railways, the National Resources Commission, the Bank of China, and the Central Bank, to name a few, did their best to develop statistics; but there was no adequate control over the collection of primary data, and the problem of reliability of the field reports was never squarely faced. Without appreciation of the importance of statistics by the central authorities, neither sufficient funds were made available nor enough competent personnel was trained.[4]

This was the situation the Chinese Communists inherited when they took over the mainland.[5] They were destined to develop a state statistical system after the Soviet model. Ineffective as the Nationalist statistical organization was, it did leave behind a few thousand employees who had some experience in statistical reporting. How did the Chinese Communists develop a national statistical system from such a meagre foundation? And with what results?

DEVELOPMENT FROM 1949 TO 1952

When the Communist government was set up in October, 1949, no effort was made to introduce a state statistical system. The place of the old Bureau of Statistics was now taken over

---

[4] What has been said about pre-1949 China should not be construed as applicable to the present situation in Taiwan, where economic planning and, therefore, statistical service have developed.

[5] For a survey of the pre-1949 statistical materials that Peiping has uncovered, see Mo Yueh-ta, Chu Hung-en, and T'ung Cheng-hui, "The so-called Statistical Legacy from Old China and the Processing of These Materials in Recent Years," *TCKT*, 16: 24–27 and 14, August, 1957. The authors reported that after the materials were "edited and utilized for making certain computations," the results have not been made available to the public because the materials "are not sufficiently complete in coverage or sufficiently reliable in quality." It may be noted that this recognition of the limitations of pre-1949 statistics has not deterred many Peiping authorities from comparing the more comprehensive post-1949 statistics with those of the 1930's in order to exaggerate the accomplishments of the new regime.

by the Department of Statistics, established under the Bureau of Planning in the Financial and Economic Commission of the Political Affairs Council (later known as the State Council). Statistical offices were also organized in the six regional administrations of the country. But, up to the end of 1952, many provinces and centrally administered cities, as well as an overwhelming majority of the local governments below the provincial level, had no such organizations; those that existed were probably inherited from the old regime. All these offices had "a staff far too small in number and too poor in quality to undertake the work in store for them." [6] The statistical services in state and state-private joint enterprises were no better. Of the six offices in the administrative regions, the one in the Northeast was the strongest. It had an early start and was headed by a trained statistician who later became one of the deputy directors of the State Statistical Bureau.[7]

The scope of statistical services during the 1949–1952 period was set forth by Li Fu-ch'un, then deputy chairman of the Financial and Economic Commission, in a speech at the First National Statistical Conference in 1951. Compilation of comprehensive and scientific statistics, he said, must begin with the state sector, only to be expanded in the direction of the semisocialist sector of coöperatives and the state-private joint enterprises. In the state sector, priority was given to industrial statistics.[8] Thus, the only major undertaking initiated by the Department of Statistics during this period was a national survey, carried out in the spring of 1950, of state and joint industrial (including mining) enterprises. These

[6] Yang Po, "Has the Direction of Our Statistical Work been Wrong?" *TCKT*, 16: 10–14, August, 1957.

[7] See Wang Szu-hua, "The Problem of Relative Importance between Industrial and Agricultural Production in the Northeast," *JMJP*, November 3, 1949, p. 5. This was a type of report that other regional statistical offices were unable to produce during the following three years. On July 9, 1961, he was appointed director of the Bureau.

[8] Yang Po, *op. cit.*

enterprises, all taken over from the previous regime, had been maintaining regular statistical reporting services for many years before 1949. But now it was found that their reporting time was not uniform, the contents of the reports and the methods of computation differed from enterprise to enterprise, and the data were "neither adequate in coverage nor accurate." [9] For the new survey, the end of 1949 was taken as the critical date, and a set of uniform schedules and computation methods was adopted. Each enterprise was requested to set up a small group, in which every department in the enterprise would be represented, to complete the returns. The results of this national survey formed the basis for drafting the first state plan of industrial rehabilitation and construction.

This period also saw the beginning of Soviet aid in statistical services. Soviet statisticians were enlisted to map the national survey, to help train statistical personnel, and to set up statistical services in the Ministries of Railways (1950) and Health (1951–52). In 1950, upon Soviet advice, the system of regular reporting with uniform statistical schedules was introduced for all major state and joint enterprises in industry and construction. During the next two years this system was extended to agriculture and internal trade, furnishing the basic data for the 1952 state economic plan.

Thus it may be said that no national statistical system had been attempted or developed during the first three years of Communist rule. Newly established statistical services were limited, and their attention was confined very much to the state and semisocialist sectors, which, according to official calculations, accounted for about 20 per cent of national income in 1952. Even these sectors were far from fully covered, because the emphasis was placed on industry. Some local surveys were probably made in the administrative regions and

[9] Ti Ch'ao-po, "Exert Effort to Complete the National Industrial Survey," *JMJP*, April 10, 1950.

large cities, since the First National Statistical Conference held in 1951 called for various undertakings.[10] Results from these surveys might well have been used as a basis for making national estimates during this period. However, when reviewing the work on statistics during these three years before the Second National Statistical Conference, the director of the new State Statistical Bureau remarked, "Too many surveys had been undertaken independently by various government departments in different areas, each varying in objective, scope, classification, tabulation, and definition."[11] It was, therefore, impossible to compile national statistics from them.

Although the first five-year plan was scheduled to start in 1953, there was actually no plan, for the only serviceable national data available to Peiping authorities pertained to the industrial output of major state and joint enterprises. If central planning was to be effected, a state statistical system had to be established promptly.

[10] The list consisted of: (1) survey of the output of major industrial products, of building activities of different government departments, and of the supply and demand of major industrial materials; (2) survey of the output and marketing of major staple food and raw materials, and of the supply and demand of fertilizer, insecticide, and the like; (3) estimate of the gross industrial and agricultural value product; (4) survey of the consumption of twenty to thirty items of daily necessities among workers, peasants and urban residents; (5) survey of population, land and natural resources; (6) import and export statistics; and (7) study of the labor force in various departments. See Yen Shou-chih, "The Correctness of our Statistical Program Permits of no Criticism," *TCKT*, 16: 22–23, August, 1957. Most of these items, impossible of immediate implementation, were merely objectives. Furthermore, the fact that foreign-trade statistics should have been included in the program implies complete disruption of the fine service that had been patiently built for a century.
[11] *JMJP*, December 29, 1952.

Part One: The Foundation

# CHAPTER II

# The State Statistical System, 1952–1957

## THE STATE STATISTICAL BUREAU

On August 8, 1952, Peiping decided to establish a state statistical bureau directly under the Political Affairs Council, with Hsüeh Mu-ch'iao in charge. The State Bureau began operation on October 1, the third anniversary of the People's Republic. According to the report of an Indian delegation that went to China in the summer of 1956, it was organized chiefly along the line of functional statistics into fifteen departments, with 611 technical and 64 nontechnical staff members, headed by a director, who was an economist, and five deputies, of whom two were statisticians and three were economists.[1] The bureau was larger than most of the central government ministries.

Hsüeh, a graduate of Tsing Hua University, is probably a Soviet-trained economist, and on the basis of his writings, he is more of an organizer. Having been secretary-general of the Financial and Economic Commission since 1949 (as well as director of the Central Bureau of Private Enterprises), he was familiar with the weaknesses of the Commission's Depart-

---

[1] The fifteen departments were: Statistics of Industry, Agriculture, Basic Construction, Trade, Distribution of Materials, Transportation and Communication, Labor and Wages, Culture, Education, Health; Comprehensive Statistics; Research, Editing, and Translating, Machine Calculation; and General Affairs. See Government of India, Ministry of Food and Agriculture, *Report of Indian Delegation to China on Agricultural Planning and Techniques*, New Delhi: 1956, pp. 82–83. Hereafter cited as *Indian Delegation Report*. Over the years the number of deputy directors varied between three and five, and was four from January, 1958, to July, 1961, when it was reduced to two.

ment of Statistics which the State Bureau now superseded and with the urgent needs for reliable data for central planning. He went about the new assignment with vigor and was able to remain in the directorship for seven years. During his tenure of office, he was also appointed to the State Planning Commission as one of its 15 members when it was first set up in November, 1952, becoming one of its senior deputy chairmen from September 1954 to August 1958. In September, 1959, he was dismissed from the State Bureau, to be replaced by one of his deputies who had been with him since 1952.

The objectives and principles that gilded the State Bureau's work from the beginning are revealed in its directives and pronouncements. First, in order to promote and facilitate the compilation of national statistics,

a centralized and unified statistical system is to be created, in which the State Bureau will be responsible for organizing all the work in statistics in the country, for standardizing methods of checking accuracy and computation, and for centralizing the distribution of all basic statistical schedules.[2]

The Soviet "pace-making experience" would be followed and should be studied by the rank and file in statistical services.[3] Second, statistical offices were to be established at all levels of local government within each province. While organizationally a part of the local governments, operationally they formed a more or less independent network with the State Bureau as the highest authority. The primary purpose of this national organization was "to render service to the task of planning" at all levels.[4] Third, statistical data should be "both

[2] "Director Hsüeh's Report at the Third National Statistical Conference," *TCKTTH*, 1: 4–11, April, 1954.

[3] "The National Conference on Statistical Work," *JMJP*, December 29, 1952.

[4] Editorial, "To Further Strengthen Statistical Work in the Period of Economic Construction," *JMJP*, March 31, 1954.

accurate and reported on time";[5] discrepant figures should be reconciled so that only one set of basic statistics would be recognized as authentic.[6] Fourth, statistical findings should be put to use. Their practical application during the period of national construction was to be fourfold: (a) as the basis for the preparation of national economic plans and a tool for supervision and inspection of their fulfillment; (b) as an aid to state leadership in the economy, especially in respect to the state control of the nonsocialist sectors and to the formulation of socializing policies; (c) as the organizer in national economic accounting, since the demand for accuracy and punctuality in statistical services would entail improvement of accounting services and business records in the same direction; and (d) as the publicizing agent for pacemakers.[7] For all these applications, mere collection and compilation of data were not enough; the final data should be studied and analyzed.[8] Through such an effort by the rank and file, the State Bureau aspired to uncover "the laws of national economic development."[9] Lastly, the training of statistical personnel was urgent. The program had to be carried out on a national scale and in such a way that a large working force would be produced within a short time.

These were ambitious objectives. Their implementation was to encounter great difficulties. In fact, many of the underlying principles were severely criticized toward the end of 1957 and in 1958. The whole statistical system was threatened with

[5] Hsu Chien, "To Service Planning is the Basic Duty of Statistical Work," *TCKTTH*, 1: 17–19, April, 1954.
[6] Hsüeh Mu-ch'iao, "Final Report at the Fourth National Statistical Conference," *TCKTTH*, 5: 1–7, May, 1955.
[7] Chiang Chao, "What are Statistics and their Functions?" *TCKTTH*, 2: 27–31, May, 1954.
[8] State Statistical Bureau, "A Directive concerning the Development of Analytical Work on Industrial Statistics," *TCKTTH*, 6: 4–6, September, 1954.
[9] "Record of Director Hsüeh's Report at the Meeting of All Bureau Workers," *TCKT*, 6: 1–6, March, 1957.

16    THE STATE STATISTICAL SYSTEM

extinction in the latter part of 1958, and was substantially revised in 1959 and 1960. How much had been achieved before the onslaught and with what results? What changes had taken place during the years of the "great leap" and with what effects on the validity of official statistics? To answer these questions, it will be convenient to divide the development into three periods, namely, 1952–1957, 1958, and 1959–1960. For each period, special attention will be paid to organization, sources of data, quality control, and personnel. An effort will be made to pinpoint the developing process chronologically in order that changes in the quality of official statistics may be traced.

ORGANIZATION

The understanding of the development of Communist China's statistical organization should be aided by a brief reference to the administrative structure of the country.

Before the advent of people's communes in the summer of 1958, the administrative structure comprised the following levels in the order of decreasing scope of authority: the center; provinces and the equivalent; special districts (*chuan ch'u*) and autonomous divisions (*tze-chih chou*); cities and *hsien;* districts (*ch'u*); towns and *hsiang;* and, finally, villages. Thus, there were six tiers at the provincial level and below. According to the constitution of 1954, local government was instituted only at the three levels of province, city and *hsien,* and town and *hsiang,* except in minority areas where "autonomous divisions" constituted another level of local government. The administrative offices at the "special districts" were an extension of the provincial government, and those at the "districts" an extension of the city or *hsien* government, while the town or *hsiang* was the primary local government in direct control of villages. Until the adoption of the constitution, there were also six administrative regional governments between the center and the provinces, each administering a number of

Table 1. STRUCTURE AND SIZE OF COMMUNIST CHINA'S LOCAL
ADMINISTRATION AT THE END OF 1953, 1957, 1958, AND 1959
(In units)

| Level | 1953 | 1957 | 1958 | 1959 |
|---|---|---|---|---|
| 1. Administrative region | 6 | 0 | 0 | 0 |
| 2. Province and equivalent | 45 | 28 | 28 | 28 |
|   a. province | 29 | 22 | 21 | 21 |
|   b. autonomous region | 1 | 2 | 4 | 4 |
|   c. special area[a] | 1 | 1 | 1 | 1 |
|   d. centrally controlled municipality | 14 | 3 | 2 | 2 |
| 3. Special district and equivalent | 164 | 171 | 160 | 160− |
|   a. special district[b] | 152 | 140[c] | 131 | .... |
|   b. autonomous division[d] | 12[e] | 31[f] | 29 | .... |
| 4. City and *hsien* | 2,287 | 2,257 | 1,930 | 1,740+ |
|   a. provincially controlled city | 152[g] | 173[f] | 183 | .... |
|   b. *hsien*[h] | 2,135 | 2,084[f] | 1,747 | .... |
| 5. People's commune | 0 | 0 | 26,578 | 24,000 |
| 6. District | 19,000 | 9,000[f] | .... | 0 |
| 7. Town and *hsiang* | 225,868 | 102,582 | .... | 0 |
|   a. town | 5,402[g] | 3,672[e] | .... | 0 |
|   b. *hsiang* | 220,466[i] | 98,910[f] | .... | 0 |
| 8. Village | [1,250,000] | .... | .... | .... |

[a] Changtu area is considered as part of Tibet area.
[b] Special districts include *meng* (a group of banners) and "administrative areas" of comparable authority.
[c] At the end of 1956.
[d] Autonomous divisions include the "autonomous districts" of comparable authority.
[e] Early 1953.
[f] At the end of April.
[g] At the end of July.
[h] Those of Tibet and Changtu are omitted.
[i] Early September, 1954, as given by Chou En-lai, "Report on the Work of the Government," *JMJP*, September 24, 1954.

SOURCES:
For 1953 and 1957, Hsüeh Yi-yuen, "The Division of Administrative Areas of the People's Republic of China," *Ti-li hseüh-pao* [Journal of Geography], 24: 84–97, February, 1958. However, the number of autonomous divisions is estimated from *1953 Jen-min shou-tse* [People's Handbook of 1953], pp. 128–148, and the number of villages is my estimate on the basis of (i) various survey reports of the 1930's and 1950's which give a population of about 400 per village, and (ii) the total village population of 505,350,000 according to the 1953 census.
For 1958, State Statistical Bureau, *Wei-ta ti shih-nien* [The Great Ten Years], Peiping, 1959, pp. 11 and 36.
For 1959, Yang Chien-pao, "On the Proportionate Relationship as the Basic Nature of a National Economy," *CCYC*, 10: 11–25, October, 1959; especially p. 23.

provinces; they formed the highest level of local government until November, 1952, when they became but an extension of the central government. In the latter half of 1954, they were abolished, one after the other. Collectivization of agriculture after the 1955 autumn harvest resulted in the enlargement of the *hsiang*, reducing heavily the number of "districts" and

towns. In the fall of 1958, when towns and *hsiang* were amal-
gamated to form people's communes, "districts" were abolished
and the number of *hsien* was somewhat reduced through
merger. The prevailing policy seems to be that *hsien* will
ultimately be replaced by communes of comparable size.

It will be recalled that before the establishment of the State
Statistical Bureau the six administrative regions and some of
the provinces had already been equipped with statistical
offices.[10] The number of offices at the provincial level was probably very small, because there was not even an office in Tientsin, the third largest centrally controlled municipality in the
country. Now the State Bureau set out to organize a network
of offices to cover every one of the five local administrative
levels. These offices were to be part of the local government
structure, but operationally subject to a straight-line command
leading up to the State Bureau itself. Starting virtually from
fresh ground, it was confronted with a gigantic organizational
task and had to proceed by stages.

At the Second National Statistical Conference convened in
December, 1952, the new director decided that statistical
offices would be set up within three months in all provinces
(except Tibet) and provincially controlled cities. This was
accomplished in May, 1953, although most of the new offices
were but skeletons. However, they began to function toward
the end of the year and consolidated their position in 1954 and
1955. By the summer of 1956, a typical provincial statistical
bureau was reported to consist of one director, one deputy
director, and a technical staff of eighty distributed among five
statistical departments (agriculture, industry, basic construction, trade and communications, and health and culture).[11]
In the cities, depending on their size, the technical staff of

---

[10] For convenience of discussion, the term "province" will be used to
include all four categories of administrative area with comparable authority.

[11] *Indian Delegation Report,* p. 83.

the statistical office was smaller. This form of organization at the provincial and city levels has probably remained much the same ever since.

Upon the completion of the provincial and city network toward the end of 1953, a drive began to establish units in all special districts and *hsien* and to install statistical workers in all districts—so as "to correct the prevailing situation in which statistical services at the *hsien* and district levels have been completely unrestrained." [12] The drive was extended to towns and *hsiang* in 1955 and 1956. A fully developed unit at the *hsien* level was either self-contained or, more commonly, placed under a joint planning and statistical division, with a technical staff of about six or eight, working on agricultural, industrial, and commercial statistics.[13] The unit at the special district level was probably not much different.

The task of setting up approximately a hundred sixty offices in the special districts was far easier than the establishment of almost a quarter of a million statistical units at the *hsien* level and below. Toward the end of the first five-year plan, the director of the State Bureau reported on the situation that in some areas where statistical units had been established at the *hsien*, district and *hsiang* levels, the services were yet to be regularized and strengthened; in some other areas where statistical units had been set up at the *hsien* level alone, their work was yet to be placed on a routine basis; and in the rest of the country there were no units established at any of these local levels.[14] Thus the whole agricultural sector continued to be serviced by a small number of part-time workers collecting statistics on which planning had to be based. The extension of the State Bureau's network to this sector was listed first in

---

[12] "Director Hsüeh's Report at the Third National Statistical Conference," *op. cit.*

[13] *Indian Delegation Report,* p. 83.

[14] "Director Hsüeh's Report at the Sixth National Statistical Conference," *TCKT,* 21: 1–21, November, 1957.

its work program for the period of the second five-year plan.

This national network of statistical offices, established by the State Bureau, constituted the so-called "state" system, in contrast to the services maintained by the regular ministries of the central government and by the "business affairs" system to be discussed presently.

# CHAPTER III

# Sources of
# Statistical Information

Neither the State Bureau nor its local offices engaged directly in field work for the purpose of collecting primary data, although occasionally working teams were dispatched to selected localities to test some techniques of investigation. The Bureau did initiate special national surveys from time to time, but its responsibility lay in designing and organizing. The regular duty of the rank and file was "to assemble, assimilate, and analyze" the statistical information received in the office and "to apply the results to checking on the implementation of state plans." [1] Through what channels did the information come to the bureau? There were three immediate sources: the government ministries and their business organizations, the primary establishments and enterprises, and the provincial and *hsien* governments.[2] Thus the validity of source data depends on the effectiveness of the statistical services operating in these sources. The bureau's concern consisted not

---

[1] State Statistical Bureau, Department of Industrial Statistics, "Basic Conclusions from Reviewing the Work on National Industrial Statistics of 1954 and the Work Program for 1955," *TCKTTH*, 9: 1–7, December, 1954; Yang Chien-pao, "Exert Effort to Develop further the Work on Comprehensive Statistics," *TCKTTH*, 5: 10–13, May, 1955.

[2] The term "primary establishment" refers to the smallest self-contained unit that has to account for its profit and loss within a similarly self-contained enterprise. For example, a state trading company is a self-contained enterprise *vis-à-vis* the state, but from 1953 through 1957, its wholesaling stations and retail stores, all over the country, were made self-contained units (primary establishments) within the company. The Anshan Iron and Steel Company is a state enterprise, with a large number of self-contained primary establishments.

only in building up these services, but in deciding on the type of data required for its own purpose and the methods of collecting them, and in devising means to control their quality and to assure a regular supply from the sources. For, what the bureau finally produced was *the* official statistics. It is necessary to look into these other statistical services.

## The "Business Affairs System"

Directly under the State Council are a number of central ministries in addition to the People's Bank and a host of commissions, bureaus, and offices. The ministries may be divided into two groups: those in charge of business affairs (such as the ministries of finance, industries, agriculture, transportation) and those in charge of nonbusiness affairs (such as the ministries of education, geology). Out of thirty-one ministries in early 1960, twenty-two belonged to the former group. With a few exceptions (foreign affairs, defense, and geology), all central ministries—either individually or jointly—have counterparts in local governments down to the city and *hsien* level; later, they were added at the level of people's communes. A line of communication is established between a ministry and its local counterparts, so that the office at the given level may communicate only with that at the next higher or lower level.

Excepting tax collection which is handled by the tax bureaus of the Ministry of Finance, the business affairs of the government are concerned with the operations of state and joint enterprises, some of which are centrally controlled, the others locally controlled, depending on the size and importance of the enterprises. Since the central ministries are preoccupied with matters of policy and administration, operational control of the centrally controlled enterprises is vested in the hands of "specialized business bureaus" or companies established under each ministry for the purpose. The local counterparts of the ministries, however, exercise direct operational control over the other group of enterprises that comes within their jurisdiction. A few examples may be cited. Since 1953 all big coal mines have been subject to the control of fifty-three bureaus of mining affairs under the Ministry of the Coal Industry, while the small mines, mostly operated by indigenous methods, are supervised directly by the Departments of Industry in the provinces and the Divisions of Industry in the city or *hsien* governments.[3] Local governments formerly had no relation with the mines run by the central bureaus, but the decentralization program beginning 1958 has given the local governments some share of control. The huge iron and steel complexes at Anshan, Pao-tou, and Wuhan are operated by the Ministry of Heavy Industry through its iron and steel companies. In internal trade, special companies were set up in 1950 under the Ministry of Trade, with branches established at different local government levels, these branches being subject to the dual control of the head offices and the local governments concerned until 1958 when they became completely locally operated units. In agriculture, there are such enterprises as state farms and ranches and tractor stations that have been operated either by the Ministry of Agriculture through its bureaus or directly by the departments or divisions of agriculture in local governments.

Each central ministry and its local counterparts includes a planning unit to which a statistical section is subordinated. In 1956, for example, the Ministry of Agriculture had a Planning Bureau with a technical staff of 76, of whom 15 constituted the Statistical Division, while the provincial government of Chekiang had a Planning Division under its Department of Agriculture employing 28 technical workers, of whom 10 worked on statistics. The same but smaller setup was found at the city and *hsien* level.[4] These statistical services were not

---

[3] Office of Statistical Materials, "The Basic Condition of China's Coal Industry," *TCYC*, 4: 18–23, April, 1958.

[4] *Indian Delegation Report*, pp. 83–84.

subject to direct operational control of the State Statistical
Bureau and its local offices. According to the directives issued
by the Political Affairs Council in 1953, they were primarily
responsible for assembling data in accordance with the needs,
methods, and standardized schedules as determined by the
State Bureau. The data collected by the local counterparts
of a ministry were, on the one hand, submitted to the cor-
responding unit at the higher level until they reached the
ministry, and on the other, transmitted to the parallel office
of the State Bureau, which, after examining them, would pass
them on to the office at the next level on up to the bureau.
The ministry and its counterparts, of course, might collect
other data to meet their own needs. However, according to
the arrangement made as early as 1954, their statistical materials should not be made available to other central and local
government agencies until the State Bureau or its local office
had processed them and given final approval to the figures.[5]
As we shall see, it took a good deal of time and effort on the
part of the bureau to implement this arrangement. The only
ministry that remains entirely outside the influence of the
bureau is that of National Defense.

The statistical services in the ministries were not so much
the concern of the bureau as those of the reporting agencies,
namely, the specialized business bureaus and companies and
the local counterparts of the ministries. These agencies together
with the People's Bank and the tax bureaus of the Ministry of
Finance constitute what is known as the "business-affairs
system" (*yeh-wu hsi-t'ung*), from which all economic statistics
originate. In 1953 the bureau succeeded in assisting most of
these operational institutions each to establish a comprehensive statistical service whose work program would be determined solely by the ministry concerned, taking into account

---

[5] State Statistical Bureau, "Replies to some Questions," *TCKTTH*,
4: 41–43, July, 1954.

the requirements of the bureau. These services soon worked well enough to enable the Bureau to prepare and issue in September, 1954, not only the first annual communique on the results of the previous year's plan, but also on the achievements in economic recovery from 1949 through 1952.[6]

The quality of statistics handled by the reporting agencies, of course, cannot be any better than the quality of data recorded in the primary establishments and the projects under construction (known as construction units). Here the State Bureau took an important step. As announced in July, 1954, the bureau through its provincial and city offices had the authority both to supervise the organization and the operation of statistical services in all state-operated enterprises and construction units and to require them to submit reports directly to the bureau in standardized schedules.[7] The bureau's leadership in this area, stressed in the work programs for 1954 and 1955, had actually begun in 1953. The difficulty encountered lay chiefly in getting a staff that would devote full time to the work and in obtaining accurate primary records. It was reported in September, 1954, that services had already been organized in state and joint industrial enterprises, particularly those centrally controlled, with a number of technical staff in each.[8] Thus the centrally controlled state enterprises in industry led the way in this development. Toward the end of 1957, Hsüeh was able to say that statistical services had been installed in practically all primary establishments in the country.[9] But the keeping of accurate primary records

[6] Deputy-Director Chia Ch'i-yun, "Report at the Fourth National Statistical Conference," *TCKTTH*, 3: 1–9, March, 1955.

[7] State Statistical Bureau, "Some Provisions concerning the Relationship in Statistical Work between Provincial and City Statistical Bureaus and Those of State-operated Enterprises and Construction Units," *TCKTTH*, 7: 13–14, October, 1954.

[8] State Statistical Bureau, "A Directive concerning the Strengthening of Industrial Statistical Work," *TCKTTH*, 6: 1–3, September, 1954.

[9] "Director Hsüeh's Report at the Sixth National Statistical Conference," *TCKT*, 21: 1–21, November, 1957.

(invoices, vouchers, tallies) remained a problem. And the improvement of the services in the establishments was listed as a major task in the bureau's work plan for the second five-year plan period—next in importance only to the introduction of statistical services in rural areas.

## THE "NONBUSINESS AFFAIRS" MINISTRIES

Not much need be said about the nonbusiness affairs ministries that form another source of statistical information for the State Bureau, because the statistical services of these ministries and their local counterparts operate the same way as those of the other ministries we have discussed. The Ministry of Health, for instance, as early as 1951 started to organize training classes for senior health administrative officers, where Soviet experts systematically presented the Soviet Union's experience in health statistical services. Ahead of most other ministries, it began in 1952 to set up a unified, standardized statistical schedule system for all health organizations in the country. In the ministry a statistical unit was organized under the Department of Planning and Finance; exact counterparts were found in the provincial governments. Throughout the years full-time or part-time workers on health statistics have been installed in special districts, cities and *hsien,* and also in hospitals, health stations, and other primary operating units.[10] The relationship between this ministerial setup and the state system of the Bureau is again the same as has been described.

This group of ministries also had under it from time to time many projects under construction, such as new schools and hospitals, all of which were regarded as basic construction units and therefore came under the direct attention of the State Bureau as far as statistical services were concerned.

---

[10] Li Kuang-yin, "Ten-Year Achievements in China's Health Statistics," *Jen-min pao-chien* [People's Health], 10: 923–926, October, 1959.

## The Private and Agricultural Sectors

Before 1953 no regular statistical coverage was attempted for private industry and trade. Estimates were made mainly on the basis of tax records and reports of state trading companies with which private enterprises were doing business. With the establishment of the State Bureau came the system of regular statistical schedules, which, although designed primarily for state and joint enterprises, was extended to cover private concerns. "Activist" elements in their employ were mobilized to see to it that they would submit accurate data. But the returns generally were found to be "unrealistic, because private enterprises were unwilling to make honest reports to the government."[11] In late 1953 when statistical offices began to function in the provinces and cities, such local government agencies as the bureaus of industry, trade, and tax collection were organized to undertake "model surveys" of private enterprises and individual craftsmen.[12] However, since samples were far from representative, the projections were not even good estimates. This prompted the State Bureau to organize the business affairs ministries and their counterparts in the provinces and cities (a) to take a census of individual craftsmen and private industrial enterprises employing more than ten persons in 1954 and (b) a census of private trade and food-and-drink catering establishments in 1955. When private industry, trade, and handicrafts were transformed into joint enterprises in 1956, the local bureaus of industry and trade were requested to readjust their statistics since 1952 on the basis of the private records now becoming available.

Before collectivization and socialization in 1956, the rural economy was predominantly private and individualistic. The

[11] "Director Hsüeh's Report at the Third National Statistical Conference," *TCKTTH*, 1: 4–11, April, 1954.

[12] For "model survey," see p. 30.

problems of collecting comprehensive data from 120 million households on agriculture, handicrafts, small trading, and rural transport were staggering. We have seen that in spite of its strenuous efforts the State Bureau failed to establish, up to 1958, regular statistical services even in the *hsien,* let alone in the towns, *hsiang,* and villages. Where and how were agricultural statistics derived?

An annual statistical report of agricultural production was nationally standardized with Soviet advice in 1951, requesting each provincial government to present a summary of farm output for the year. In fact, from 1949 to 1952 the *hsien* government was generally responsible for preparing agricultural reports for the provincial government which in turn transmitted them to the central government. Before reports were made, the *hsien* government was expected to consult its records and conduct investigations. As far as records are concerned, the data on cultivated area and rural population had probably been improved as a result of land redistribution. The effects of land reform on rural statistics, however, should not be overstated, because subsequently the State Bureau has not been able, in its nation-wide search, to gather enough materials to present a comprehensive, statistical picture of the movement.[13] In any case, to ascertain current agricultural data requires investigation. According to a party member who spoke from personal experience, investigations were made during this period by cadres in the field, who generally gave fictitious accounts. And when reports were prepared in the *hsien* government,

the Bureau of Agriculture, in order to show its achievements, tended to submit high production and low disaster-affected area figures, whereas the opposite was true with the Food Bureau, the Finance Division, and the Relief Office. Thus not only the

---

[13] Chia Ch'i-yun, "Several Problems in the Present Reform Movement of Statistical Services," *TCKT,* 15: 5–10, August, 1958.

cadres at the primary levels fabricated figures, but the *hsien* government itself indulged in pure guesswork and fabrication.[14]

Although this was a description for a particular area in Hopei province, it was quite representative of the general situation.

Beginning in 1953, however, the State Bureau introduced a regular reporting system of agricultural production schedules. They were sent to provincial governments in consolidated forms, no separate tabulation forms being made available to those governments under the provincial level.[15] Provincial governments were expected, however, to have the lower-level governments conduct investigations in accordance with the requirements set forth in the schedules. To fill out these schedules required the following within a year: (a) one or several investigations of sown area and crops harvested, according to actual production conditions of the area; (b) one investigation of the output of tea, silkworms, and fruits in major producing locations; and (c) a census of livestock, cultivated area, and mutual-aid teams and producers' coöperatives. Returns had to be made upon the completion of each investigation. In addition, there was the annual return that summarized the results of the year with correction when necessary. The number of reports each year varied from ten to fifteen according to the different agricultural conditions of an area. During the period of collectivization, from July 1955 to March 1957, a monthly report was also requested on the number of collectives, the number of participating households, the amount of cultivated area, and the number of nonparticipating households.[16]

---

[14] Li Chi-p'ing, "How has the Party Directed and Utilized Statistical Services?" *TCKT*, 13: 7–13, July, 1958.

[15] Hsüeh Mu-ch'iao, "Report at the National Meeting on Agricultural Statistical Work," *TCKT*, 22: 7–11, November, 1957.

[16] Huang Chien-t'o, "Exert Effort to Improve Agricultural Statistical Services," *TCKT*, 8: 5–8, April, 1957.

It was in pace with this development of regular reporting that toward the end of 1953, the State Bureau made a drive to establish statistical units in special districts and *hsien* and to install statistical workers in all districts.[17] To start the system working under these limiting conditions, the State Bureau suggested that for 1953 and 1954 surveys should center on food crops and cotton. The method of investigation was that of model survey in which the investigator chose a few samples considered in his judgment to be typical of the situation. It differs from scientific sampling in that the size of its sampling is much smaller and its choice of samples is subject to personal bias. "Our method of collecting statistical materials," said the State Bureau's senior deputy director, "will be chiefly that of estimating on the basis of model surveys." [18] Since the investigators were designated to be either mutual-aid teams, agricultural coöperatives, or cadres in the *hsiang* and village, the "models" chosen for investigation were most likely some of the mutual-aid teams and coöperatives themselves that were more willing and ready to furnish data than family farms. Moreover, when reports from the *hsien* were all assembled in the provincial government, it "adjusted and supplemented" the figures (with such other information as food procurements by state trading agencies) before submitting them to the central authorities. Hence, the provincial totals did not agree with the sums of the figures at the *hsien* level.[19]

By 1955, however, it was reported that in many areas statistical committees had been set up at the *hsiang* level or below to assist in investigation. This type of committee was usually composed of not only local officers of the tax, food, trade, and education bureaus, but representatives of women

[17] See above, p. 19.
[18] "Chia Ch'i-yun's Concluding Report at the National Agricultural Statistical Conference," *TCKTTH*, 1: 5–8, January, 1955.
[19] Hsüeh Mu-ch'iao, "Final Report at the Fourth National Statistical Conference," *TCKTTH*, 5: 1–7, May, 1955.

organizations and primary-school graduates. While the chief administrative officer of the area (a district, *hsiang,* or village) served as chairman of the committee, it was his secretary, usually a party member, who was charged with the primary responsibility of preparing the returns. These preliminary returns, however, had to be reviewed, adjusted, and approved by the local party and government leaders at each level before they were submitted to the next higher level. This was necessary, according to the official explanation, because these leaders had a broader knowledge of the agricultural situation than the committees.

With the widespread organization of this type of committee in the rural areas, the State Bureau was able to place definite responsibilities on different local governments in 1955. Sown area was to be estimated by mutual-aid teams and local cadres in the *hsiang* and villages according to their own records and observation; investigation household by household was not necessary. Crops harvested were to be estimated by the *hsien* government on the basis of model surveys that it should conduct. Output of fruits, tea leaves, and silkworms was to be reported by major producing areas. Data on livestock, cultivated area, and population were to be gathered by cadres in the *hsiang* and villages. Materials on forestry and water conservation were to be reported by the special district and *hsien* governments. Finally, output data on aquatic products should be collected by the appropriate local government bureau in the producing areas—either directly from state-operated enterprises or from model surveys of fishery coöperatives.[20]

With collectivization in 1956 and 1957, the picture did not change much. The bookkeepers of agricultural collectives

[20] State Statistical Bureau, Department of Agricultural Statistics, "The Program of Agricultural Statistical Work for 1955," *TCKTTH,* 1: 8–11, January, 1955.

were included in the membership of the statistical committees at the *hsiang* level. Two additional sets of schedules were introduced in 1956, namely the basic rural statistical report and the report for agricultural producer coöperatives. The collectives made their own returns for the *hsiang* government, based on the reports from the component work units. The *hsiang* government prepared a separate comprehensive report on basic agricultural and rural conditions for the whole area, and submitted it, together with the returns from the collectives, to the district and the *hsien* governments, each of which consolidated all these reports and adjusted them according to their own judgment.

Alongside this development of agricultural statistics, the State Bureau also attempted to gather other types of data on the rural economy. In 1956 a study of land for major agricultural uses other than crop land was initiated. Moreover, from 1955 to 1958, it organized two series of national surveys: one on income and its distribution in agricultural coöperatives and collectives, and the other on family budgets of agricultural and industrial workers. The former was a "model survey," but the latter was claimed to be the first scientifically conceived "sample survey" undertaken in the country.[21]

How did this system of collecting agricultural statistics work out? During these years since 1953, the returns were late and deficient, and the surveys and reports of agricultural villages and collectives were "gravely disorderly."[22] In the collectives, bookkeeping, not to mention statistical services, was very poorly done, and a large number of those reporting underreported output and omitted in their returns the cultivated

[21] For the State Bureau's agricultural statistical work program for 1956, see *Nung-yeh t'ung-chi kung-tso shou-tse* [Handbook for Agricultural Statistical Work], Peiping, June, 1956. The full text has been translated by the United States Consulate General, Hong Kong, in *Current Background* (mimeographed), no. 434, January 15, 1957.

[22] Huang Chien-t'o, "Exert Effort to Improve Agricultural Statistical Services," *TCKT*, 8: 5–8, April, 1957.

land retained by their members.[23] At the end of 1957, the
director of the State Bureau reported that while some provinces were able to complete their statistical schedules according to the consolidated reports from the lower levels, there
were still many others where groundless estimates were made
at each level of local government without the benefit of field
reports.[24] The key to the situation lay in the *hsien* government. But, "strictly speaking," said Hsüeh in April, 1958, "agricultural statistical services and statistical organization at
the *hsien* level have not been installed in the great majority
of areas up to the present. The *hsien* government still does not
have any experience in handling statistical work." [25] Throughout the 1953–1957 period, the State Bureau tried in vain
to establish a network of statistical units, vertically subject to its authority, to take charge of agricultural statistics.[26]
Agricultural statistical services had failed even to grow roots
in the rural area.[27] In Hsüeh's words, "we are not even clear
about such important agricultural questions as the size of
territorial area, and the amount of cultivated land." [28]

We have seen that local agricultural bureaus had tended to
inflate agricultural production statistics in order to show
their achievements. There must have long been a sharp conflict between the Ministry of Agriculture (and its local counterparts) and the State Bureau on the jurisdiction over agri-

---

[23] "Joint Panel Discussion between the State Statistical Bureau and
the Ministry of Agriculture on the Method of Surveying Crops Harvested," *TCKT*, 17: 27, September, 1957; and, Hsüeh Mu-ch'iao, "Report at the National Meeting on Agricultural Statistical Work," *TCKT*,
22: 7–11, November, 1957.

[24] Hsüeh, *ibid.*

[25] Hsüeh Mu-ch'iao, "To establish a Unified Control System of Agricultural Statistical Service is the Road to Develop Statistical Work in
the *Hsien*," *TCKT*, 8: 1–4, April, 1958.

[26] Huang Chien-t'o, *op. cit.*

[27] Hsüeh Mu-ch'iao, "Report at the National Meeting on Agricultural
Statistical Work," *TCKT*, 22: 7–11, November, 1957.

[28] *Ibid.*

cultural statistics, for at the end of the first five-year plan, Hsüeh outspokenly insisted that agricultural collectives, unlike the state-operated farms and ranches, were properly within the bureau's province.[29] As mentioned before, organization of statistical services at the *hsien* level and below was listed as the first item in the bureau's work program for the period of the second five-year plan. In fact, the bureau planned to start in 1958 sending statistical schedules not only to the provincial governments as before, but directly (through its provincial and city bureaus) to the *hsien* governments, and in some areas, also to the agricultural collectives. During the second five-year period, the method of investigation was expected to change more and more from that of model survey to that of crop-cutting sample survey. Nevertheless, because this new method would take a long time to be adopted generally, Hsüeh pointed out that

for many years to come, we still have to rely on the party and government authorities at different levels of local government, who are more familiar with the local agricultural situation, to check and adjust—with the aid of other materials at their disposal (such as the amount of state procurement)—the agricultural output data gathered by local statistical workers.[30]

---

[29] *Ibid.*

[30] "Director Hsüeh's Report at the Sixth National Statistical Conference," *op. cit.*

CHAPTER IV

# Quality Control

On January 8, 1953, the Political Affairs Council issued a
directive on statistical organization and services that laid the
foundation of a state statistical system, authorizing the State
Bureau to control the collection and quality of statistical data
in the country. It ordered local governments of different levels,
central and local agencies and enterprises of the business-
affairs system and joint enterprises to comply with all statistical regulations and methods of the State Bureau and to
complete the statistical schedules the State Bureau issued.
It added that while to fill out the returns not in accordance
with the regulations might be subject to disciplinary action,
"to report fictitious or false statistical figures and materials
would be under severe penalty as a dishonest act against the
state." [1] With this broad authority, the State Bureau set out
to develop three operational systems all aiming at control over
the quality of data: the unified regular statistical schedules,
the unified "statistical computation checking" system, and the
centralized control and supply of basic national statistics.

THE UNIFIED SYSTEM OF REGULAR SCHEDULES

Introduced in 1950 with Soviet advice, the system of regular
schedules became the basic device for the State Bureau to
gather statistical information. As it developed, the system not
only implied standardization of definitions, classifications,

---

[1] Quoted in "Director Hsüeh's Report at the Sixth National Statistical
Conference," *TCKT*, 21:1–21, November, 1957.

36

computing methods, national indicators, and methods of investigation, but it entailed centralization of authority in the construction and distribution of statistical schedules.

Definitions, classifications, computing methods, and indicators require separate treatment for each of the functional statistical fields. A few comments will have to suffice. Soon after the State Bureau started to operate in October, 1952, it formulated, in coöperation with the State Planning Commission, the list of "1952 constant prices" for industrial and agricultural products; the timing of the formulation probably explains why these constant prices were averages of market prices in the third quarter of the year. At the same time, a set of national indicators was drawn up together with the method of computing them. These indicators defined not only what should be construed as targets in planning for different fields, but the type of statistics required and the way in which they should be computed and recorded. For example, twelve indicators were used in industrial planning and statistics from 1953 through 1957, such as total value of production, physical output of major products, average wages, total wage bill, labor force, profits, labor productivity, and cost reduction. Each of these required precise definition, and, for the purpose of compiling national statistics, admitted of one uniform method of computation and classification. The compilation, with Soviet aid, of a unified catalogue of commodities, which came in use in 1955, is an example of the ramifications.[2] It is, indeed, not inaccurate to say that the State Bureau's work on standardization of statistical procedures was entirely related to the development of national indicators and that these indicators constituted what the State Bureau considered as "basic national statistics."

[2] For catalogue, see State Statistical Bureau, Department of Trade Statistics, "Explanations of Some Problems Concerning the Unified Catalogue of Commodities in Internal Trade," *TCKTTH*, 9: 38–41, December, 1954.

Some of the standardized procedures were later revised as a result of difficulties in practical application, but the change was mostly in the direction of refinement—a sharper definition rather than a new definition. The greatest source of difficulty in enforcement came from the planning authorities, who kept employing in their work, concepts of the indicators and methods of computation and classification that did not agree with those of the State Bureau. Only after the middle of 1955 when the State Planning Commission came to the support of the bureau's policy did uniformity begin to develop.[3] Another difficulty lay in the technical nature of some indicators; this, coupled with the lack of training of statistical workers, made much of the computation meaningless, and goes far to explain why official statistics on costs, wages, and labor force, for example, have been either inadequate or unavailable.

The regular statistical schedules, composed primarily of national indicators, were of three types: annual, quarterly, and monthly. For state, joint, and coöperative enterprises (agricultural coöperatives excepted), annual schedules were considered to be of basic importance, because the returns had to be made by all units in the business affairs and nonbusiness affairs systems (except the military), thus constituting a complete count in the country. Complete enumeration is a principle to which the State Bureau held steadfastly throughout the period, and the annual schedules, in which the principle was embodied, "are the most important basis of our entire statistics."[4] At the beginning, only the important enterprises could comply; but, as the State Bureau began to make determined efforts to organize and improve the statistical services in all state enterprises and basic construction units, especially after July, 1954, the coverage rapidly widened. On

[3] Hsia Szu-p'ing, "Statistical Work in Recent Years as Viewed from Planning," *TCKT*, 17: 17–18, September, 1957.

[4] "Director Hsüeh's Report at the Sixth National Statistical Conference," *op. cit.*

the other hand, the quarterly and monthly schedules were designed to cover only major enterprises in the important cities, the returns being used as much for checking on their implementation of the state plan as for estimating national progress. For example, in 1953 and 1954 only 20 per cent of the state-operated industrial enterprises were required to file telegraphically the monthly schedules, but they represented more than 80 per cent of the total value product of the whole group. As for private industrial and trading enterprises, annual and quarterly or monthly returns were demanded of only the large-sized enterprises in about twenty cities, whose value product accounted for 80 per cent of the total. For minor private industrial concerns, individual craftsmen, small trading, and agriculture, regular returns (chiefly annual, except agriculture) were made by local governments on the basis of model surveys. Recognizing the great margin of error in these estimates, the State Bureau, as we have seen, organized national surveys "to supplement the deficiencies in the regular returns." [5]

While the State Bureau was concerned with national indicators in the regular schedules, other central and provincial government agencies wanted data for administrative, operating, and planning purposes. As a result, all primary establishments and the governments at the *hsien* and *hsiang* levels in particular were flooded with all sorts of tabulation forms. Often asking the same kind of questions, they competed with the regular schedules for the time of those who had to fill them out, thus delaying the return of the schedules, creating confusion about the meaning of indicators as diverse definitions were used by different agencies, and, above all, inducing careless entries. In 1954, the State Bureau reaffirmed in detail its central authority, conferred by the Political Affairs Council,

---

[5] "Record of Director Hsüeh's Report at the Meeting of All Bureau Workers," *TCKT*, 6: 1–6, March, 1957.

to approve or distribute all statistical schedules and forms
drawn up by central ministries for their local counterparts and
for enterprises under their control. Even in regard to the
standard forms for business accounting that were the concern
of the Ministry of Finance, the State Bureau's approval would
have to be secured so that the content, including indicators,
would be in line with that of the statistical schedules. Provincial governments were given no authority to devise and
distribute statistical questionnaires. However, the State Bureau had had little success in enforcing this authority either
at the central or at the local level, although it sought and
received support from the party in 1955. Not unexpectedly,
resentment came from the ministries, which finally in 1957
regained the authority to design schedules for enterprises
under their control, with the result that the growing number
of schedules rendered the preparation of consolidated statistics
difficult. The situation in rural areas was never brought under
control. In spite of the bureau's avowed attempt to start in
1956 unifying all statistical questionnaires sent by various
agencies to the countryside, the flow of these inquiries "had
turned into a deluge" by 1957.[6]

With this effort to build a unified system of regular schedules with standardized statistical procedures, the general use
of a uniform set of weights and measures was vital to the
State Bureau's scheme but entirely beyond its control. The
"market" system of weights and measures, long adopted by
the previous regime to take the place of the traditional system,
was accepted by the Communist government in 1949, for
which a central bureau was established. From 1950 to 1952
the number of local offices increased from thirty to more
than one hundred and twenty, and according to an incomplete
count, the number of plants producing the standard equip-

---

[6] Wang Szu-hua, "On a Great Contradiction in China's Statistical
Work at the Present," *TCKT*, 15: 8–11, August, 1957.

ment grew from 1,400 to 2,500.[7] The plant in Peiping was soon
enlarged to become the largest in the country, beginning production in May, 1954. However, for convenience in economic
planning, the metric system has also been used since 1953
alongside the "market" system. A long debate concerning the
advisability of adopting the metric system followed, and was
not resolved until June, 1959, when the State Council decided
on the adoption of it as the legal system—without eliminating
the "market" system.[8] What is relevant in this development to
the present discussion is that many of the medium- and small-
sized establishments, whether state, joint or private, had no
standard equipment; in some instances no equipment of any
kind for weights and measures was available, business accounts being kept on the basis of personal estimates by the
management. In rural areas the situation was worse: the habit
of using the old system lingered on, and most of the equipment
in use was defective.

## The "Unified Statistical Computation Checking" System

The term "computation checking" in Chinese (*ho-suan*) car-
ries the meaning of auditing, checking, and calculation, and
is clearly intended to be the Chinese equivalent of the Soviet
term *uchet* that has no exact English equivalent. Professor
Gregory Grossman has suggested "recording" or "keeping of
records" as the nearest translation instead of "accounting"
as generally adopted.[9] But the term "keeping of records" does
not accurately describe the content of the term in Chinese
without an explanation. According to what has been published
in Communist China on the subject, "computation" or "check
on computation" seems the most appropriate. "Computation"
is used here as something far more complicated than a mere

---

[7] *TKP*, August 22, 1953.
[8] *JMJP*, July 2, 1959.
[9] See the discussion in Gregory Grossman, *Soviet Statistics of Physical
Output of Industrial Commodities*, New Jersey: Princeton University
Press, 1960, pp. 9–10, and footnote on pp. 15–16.

adding or multiplying; it means the choice of proper prices and proper methods to calculate certain well-defined indicators. Of course, computation is made for the sake of recording. If "recording" is defined to mean "recording with proper methods of computation," it may be used as an abbreviation.

The so-called unified statistical computation checking system is designed to raise the quality of statistics and to improve the statistical services at all levels. What it involves has been succinctly explained by Hsüeh:

> In socialist countries, statistical computation is generally built on the computations for financial accounts and for operation records. For the sake of facilitating statistical computation of the national economy and utilizing statistical materials for operational control, uniformity in computation methods for statistical, financial accounting, and operation records must be striven for as far as possible. Only through this effort will a unified computation system for the national economy be established.[10]

Hence, a unified statistical computation system requires, first, uniformity in computation methods within the statistical services, and then uniformity between the statistical services and the business-affairs agencies.[11]

The device for attaining uniformity within the statistical services, first introduced in 1953, is known as the "double-tracked" method, very similar to what has long been in use in the Soviet Union. In essence, it requires that each state-operated or joint enterprise prepare two copies of statistical returns, one to be submitted to the controlling agency, and

---

[10] "Director Hsüeh's Report at the Sixth National Statistical Conference," *op. cit.* In Soviet terminology, "statistical computation" or "computation for statistical records" is *statisticheskii uchet;* "computation for financial accounts," *bukhgalterskii uchet;* "computation for operation records," the combination of *operativnyi uchet* and *teckhnicheskii uchet,* referring to operational and engineering recording; and "computation system for the national economy," *narodnokhoziaistvennyi uchet.*

[11] Hsüeh Mu-ch'iao, "Final Report at the Fourth National Statistical Conference," *TCKTTH,* 5: 1–7, May, 1955.

the other to the local statistical office. These latter agencies and offices will each consolidate the returns, and, through proper channels, submit them to the State Bureau, where figures will be finalized after comparing and checking the consolidated returns. More specifically, the scheme operates as follows:[12]

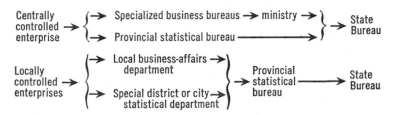

It will be observed that comparing and checking are done at the State Bureau in the first case and at the provincial bureau in the second. As practiced in China during this period, this scheme applied only to those statistical returns that presented a summary of the results of national economic construction. All other returns were submitted in single copies either through the business-affairs hierarchy or through the statistical administration. Moreover, even in 1954, a large number of state and joint enterprises remained outside this system because of their inability to comply.[13]

As officially explained, this double-channeling served the purpose of both reinforcing supervision over statistical work and giving assurance to the reliability of statistical materials. However, it also empowered the controlling agencies at each level of review to adjust the figures—theoretically according to their best judgment. We have seen that this had been consistently done in regard to agricultural statistics. And it was

[12] Tien Ch'i, "The Double-Tracked System," *TCKTTH*, 5: 41, May, 1956.

[13] Huang Hai, "Several Problems on Regular Industrial Statistical Schedules," *TCKTTH*, 1: 23–27, April, 1954.

probably no less true for other statistics. Obviously to allay resentment among the rank and file, the chief of the Department of Industrial Statistics in the State Bureau wrote,

The view held by some people that the system of review by the party and official leadership will give no assurance to the objectivity of statistical figures is incorrect or not entirely correct. On the contrary, this measure is necessary to insure the quality of statistics under the present condition of statistical services, because, with better knowledge of ideology and a much more thorough knowledge of the total situation than statistical workers have, the leadership is able to tell the false from the true.[14]

That the view referred to had to be officially admitted as "not entirely correct" indicates that much of the intervention was arbitrary.

By double-channeling of returns, however, the State Bureau did attempt to counteract this tendency. The following remark, made by the chief of the Department of Comprehensive Statistics in the State Bureau, is illuminating:

Statistical figures in the possession of the state statistical organization are generally returns from the business-affairs agencies, and may be considered as final figures as soon as they have been reviewed by the statistical organization. However, certain figures, such as those for agriculture and handicrafts, are generally arrived at through model survey—with a low degree of reliability. Different estimates could result, in which case the statistical agency will have, first, to review them together with the control agency concerned in order to reach agreement, and then to submit them to the party and the government at the appropriate level for approval.

With regard to certain figures upon which agreement can not be reached, the statistical and the control agencies must submit to a decision either by the statistical office at the next higher level or by the party and the government at that level. In the latter case, if the statistical agency does not agree with the decision of

[14] Wang I-fu, "Struggle for Improving the Accuracy of Industrial Statistical Figures," *TCKTTH*, 3: 15–17, March, 1955.

the party and the government, it may reserve its position and report to the statistical office at the next higher level. This is proper because *statistical figures reflect objective reality and should never yield to subjective wishes.*[15]

It may be added that disagreement between the State Bureau and a ministry would have to be settled by the office of the State Council in the charge of a deputy premier, where are grouped together the State Planning Commission, the State Economic Commission (since 1956), the State Statistical Bureau, and several other commissions and bureaus. In any case, the figures for important indicators would not become final until approved by the State Council, while finalization of the others required consultation with the State Planning and State Economic Commissions. Frequent as the intervention by party and government leaders at different levels must have been, no indication can be found as to the extent of arbitrariness imposed on finalized figures.

It will also be observed that double-channeling of returns provided no checking at the level of enterprise, where all statistical reports originated. Overreporting of production and underreporting of materials in store were too tempting to be resisted, because, when undetected, they would result in awards and bonuses. The Dairen Spinning and Weaving Mill, a centrally controlled state enterprise, was a case in point. There the planning unit, established in the enterprise, was charged with the responsibility of checking the performance according to the state plan and certifying statistical returns. But through the connivances of management and part of the labor force, the mill consistently overreported output until 1954. Various devices were used, such as increasing the weight of bags by watering and soiling, and putting wood or empty tubes into them. The weight scale was defective.

---

[15] Yang Chien-pao, "Exert Effort to Develop further the Work on Comprehensive Statistics," *TCKTTH*, 5: 10–13, May, 1955. Italics mine.

Statistical workers and tallying clerks were careless in their recording. The planning unit was unable to check all these malpractices, nor did it insist on certifying statistical reports before they were submitted to the control agency above. As a result, the mill received honors and bonuses.[16] From the State Bureau's viewpoint, effective checking depended a great deal on making all records of planning, statistics, finance, and operation comparable to one another.

Uniformity in computation methods between the statistical services and the business-affairs agencies was discussed at the Fourth National Statistical Conference in 1955. There, Hsüeh pointed out that uniformity in computing methods between statistical recording, financial accounting, and operational recording would be difficult to achieve within one or two years because of the low level of managing ability in enterprises. He suggested, however, that "models" might be chosen from various types of business enterprises for experimentation. Although how far this experiment was carried out has not been reported, the State Bureau in the following year, when all private enterprises were socialized, received enough central support and was sufficiently confident itself to put through a definite program: (a) all regulations on computation and recording as issued by the Ministry of Finance and the State Bureau were to be made generally uniform in 1956; (b) before the end of 1957 all business-affairs agencies and the enterprises under their control were to make their computing methods uniform in accordance with the regulations of the Ministry of Finance and the State Bureau; (c) beginning in 1956 computing methods in industry, basic construction, trade, and transportation were gradually to be made uniform with reference to statistical schedules, preliminary and realized

---

[16] Ministry of the Textile Industry, Dairen Spinning and Weaving Mill, "How Has My Mill Eliminated Fictitious Figures on Output and Efficiency?" *TCKTTH*, 7: 31–33, October, 1954.

budgets, and financial accounts; and, (d) the controlling agencies should see to it that in each enterprise under their control the keeping of primary records be improved and computation for statistical, financial, and operation records be gradually made uniform—with the objective that the method of computing important indicators be the same in all major enterprises in 1956 and in all large-sized enterprises in 1957.[17]

It is noteworthy that Hsüeh was able to say before the rank and file of the State Bureau in February, 1957, "In the last few years the unified statistical computation checking system has basically been established."

CENTRALIZED CONTROL AND SUPPLY
OF BASIC NATIONAL STATISTICS

One of the most serious problems confronting the State Bureau in the early years was the confusion and inconsistency in statistics. For planning and operational control, widely discrepant figures were adopted by different agencies at the same level of government as well as among different levels. Such confusion, according to an official explanation, resulted from differences in scope, depth, definition, and computing method among the schedules issued by the planning, statistical, and controlling authorities.[18] But even in upward reporting within any one administrative hierarchy, contradictory statistics were frequently submitted. The double-tracked methods of review, introduced in 1953, would have yielded unified statistical figures, had all state and joint enterprises been brought into the scheme in time. However, even if the State Bureau had been able to do so, the business-affairs ministries and departments most probably would not as yet have had sufficient confidence in the bureau's work to accept its figures.

---

[17] "National Program for Statistical Work, 1956–1957," *TCKTTH*, 11: 1–3, June, 1956.

[18] Editorial, "Raise the Level of Statistical Work from the Present Base!" *TCKTTH*, 1: 1–4, January, 1955.

It was against this background that in March, 1954, the State Council authorized the State Bureau to centralize the control and supply of basic national statistics, with the obligation to insure the accuracy of each figure supplied. This directive lay the foundation for the system of unifying statistical figures and centralizing their supply to the planning authorities at different levels.

In unification of figures, the State Bureau's policy was to enable the statistical organization and the business-affairs agencies at central and all local government levels to arrive at identical statistics for important indicators. A series of measures was issued in 1954, clarifying the definitional and classificational matters contained in the regular statistical schedules; and in early 1955 a set of regulations governing the procedure of revising figures was put in force. Unification was achieved first in industrial statistics before the end of 1954. But the development in other types of statistics was slower and called for a major effort on the part of the Department of Comprehensive Statistics. By the latter half of 1955 unification was generally achieved; the subject was no longer under discussion. Significantly, the effort of the Department of Comprehensive Statistics in 1955 was directed to unifying not only current statistical figures but the "final" figures for important indicators since 1949.[19]

Unification was extended also to the public use of statistics. In 1954 the State Council enunciated a number of principles governing the publication of national economic statistics in newspapers and magazines. In essence, publication of figures not approved by the statistical authorities was forbidden under the penalty of public criticism. The statistical organization was given the responsibility of certifying, before publication, all statistical figures used in newspaper editorials, statements and speeches by responsible officials, dispatches on

[19] Yang Chien-pao, *op. cit.*

fulfillment of national or local plans, or propaganda literature for foreign countries. If figures were published without prior certification and turned out to be wrong, correction must be made in a subsequent issue, and criticism of the practice raised. Judging from the publications since the latter part of 1954, this measure had been carried through effectively. It is worth noting that as a result national data found in various publications should be as "official" as those issued by the State Bureau.

As for the centralized supply of statistics, the chief difficulty stemmed from the planning authorities at different levels who continued to gather data directly from the business-affairs agencies even after the State Council's directive of March, 1954.[20] On the State Bureau's appeal, the State Planning Commission issued two instructions later in the year, the more important of which, dated August 24, provided that for the supply or certification of statistical materials, the Planning Commission itself would henceforth depend on the State Bureau, the ministries on their statistical departments, and the provincial governments on the local statistical bureaus, and that the statistical administration must furnish in time all basic statistics to the planning and business-affairs-controlling agencies at various levels.[21] Again, the industrial ministries and their hierarchy were the first to comply before the end of 1954. But as late as February, 1956, the *People's*

---

[20] It should be realized, however, that since November 15, 1952 when the establishment of the State Planning Commission was decided upon (with Kao Kang as chairman), it had been subject directly to the chairman of the government, and not to the jurisdiction of the Political Affairs Council. Only since September, 1954, has the commission been placed under the State Council when the latter was organized under the new constitution to take the place of the Political Affairs Council. See Wang Kwong-wei, "The Tasks of the State Planning Commission," *CHCC*, 2: 11–14, February, 1956.

[21] State Planning Commission, "Unified Regulations concerning certain Problems in Planning and Statistical Work," *TCKTTH*, 7: 11–12, October, 1954.

*Daily* in an editorial still found it necessary to remind the ministries that they should issue neither statistics nor schedules to those agencies outside their own administrations.[22] It may be noted, however, that since only the supply of basic statistics was centralized, there must be a mass of other data gathered by the business-affairs agencies for the purpose of operational control that did not come within the purview of the state statistical services.

Publication of national economic statistics beginning the latter half of 1955 owed much to this centralized system of control and supply. The amount of materials accumulated in the State Bureau became so vast that under the Department of Comprehensive Statistics an Office of Statistical Materials was set up in 1956, in whose name many valuable national statistical summaries were later published in the official journal of the bureau.[23] During the "free discussion" period in early 1957, the State Bureau was severely taken to task for withholding publication of all the national statistics in its hands. Hsüeh's reply deserves attention:

Concerning the supply of statistical materials, we are not satisfied ourselves and are making an effort to improve. In the past the supply did not amount to much; but it has been increasing for a year and will certainly continue to increase. The main reason for this limited supply is not found in keeping the materials secret (although no one would object to the keeping of state secrets), but in their incompleteness and insufficient accuracy. They need to be carefully checked, studied, and supplemented. Only when becoming sufficiently accurate and reliable will they be officially released. This, indeed, is our attitude in taking conscientiously the responsibility toward the people and toward statistical work.[24]

---

[22] *JMJP*, February 22, 1956.

[23] For a description and detailed classification of the materials in the State Bureau, see Tung Shao-hua, "Our Work in Taking Care of Statistical Materials," *TCKTTH*, 19: 31–33, October, 1956.

[24] Hsüeh Mu-ch'iao, "Statistical Workers must Rise to Struggle against the Rightists," *TCKT*, 16: 1–4, August, 1957.

There is some truth in the statement, because Communist China was much more generous in publishing national statistics during this period than the Soviet Union had ever been until several years after Stalin's death. But whether all the statistics published by the State Bureau were "sufficiently accurate and reliable" is open to serious question.

CHAPTER V

# Personnel and Training

Since October, 1952, the working force in statistics had grown
in pace with the rapid spread of the state statistical network
over the country and the accompanied development of statistical services in the business-affairs system. In the state statistical organization alone, the working force in the central
office and the provincial and city bureaus claimed about 4,000
at the end of 1953, with more than 10,000 in the special districts, *hsien,* and local districts; the total increased to about
20,000 in May, 1950, and reached "several tens of thousands"
in October, 1957. The working force in the business-affairs
ministries and agencies and in the state and joint enterprises
about doubled from May, 1954 (80,000) to October, 1957.
During the same period of three and a half years, the number
of statistical workers in the whole country had grown from
100,000 to nearly 200,000—not counting those in rural areas
who, while remaining in their "productive" pursuits, volun-
teered to do statistical work without pay, or those who kept
records in workshops or mining fields. Presumably, workers
in the state statistical services were all full-time, whereas part
of the working force in the business-affairs system, especially
in the enterprises, were part-time workers.

What was the quality of this working force? As pointed
out by the State Bureau in May, 1954, "an overwhelming majority of the national statistical working force never had any
special training in statistics, lacking any knowledge in statis-

tical work or economic construction, remaining at a rather low level of political ideology." [1] Training, therefore, had to be given everywhere to the workers on the job, who would attend, by groups in rotation, short courses of a few months' duration or periodical lectures and discussions. Coaching stations were developed in rural areas. Instruction centered on the operation of the statistical system, the recording methods related to schedules, and the working programs and other related documents. In the business-affairs agencies the short courses placed emphasis on the problems of functional statistics. The rank and file were required to subscribe, in groups, to the official journal of the State Bureau and to organize discussion on articles of importance to their work. Instructors were chosen from college professors, school teachers, high-school and college graduates, and those in the statistical or professional services who had some theoretical or specialized training. All senior officers from the central to the provincial and city levels, whether in the state system or in the business-affairs system, were assigned to study the *Principles of Statistics* (1953 ed.) published by the Soviet Central Statistical Administration.[2] In the summer of 1956, an Indian delegation observed that in the State Bureau and the provincial and city bureaus, senior statisticians usually had four years of training in college while others generally had one year of training organized by the bureau. Workers at the *hsien* level were given three to four months' training organized by the provincial bureau; those at the *hsiang* level attended periodical lectures.[3]

---

[1] "Strengthen the Training and Education of Statistical Workers," *TCKTTH*, 2: 1–2, May, 1954.

[2] State Statistical Bureau, "A Directive Concerning Specialized Statistical Training of On-the-Job Workers," *TCKTTH*, 5: 8–9, May, 1955; and, State Statistical Bureau, Department of Education, "Some Problems of Improving the Statistical Training Courses," *TCKT*, 3: 26–27, February, 1957.

[3] *Indian Delegation Report*, p. 83.

The training program met with many difficulties. The training period was generally too short to be effective. In 1957, the State Bureau suggested a training period of one year for junior statistical officers with 20-hour weekly class instruction, and a period of six months for the rank and file with 24-hour weekly class instruction. More serious was the shortage of instructors, most of whom could not give full time to the program. Teaching facilities and reading materials were lacking. Perhaps most serious was the rate of turnover in the working force and the quality of the trainees. Since many statistical workers in enterprises and almost all in rural areas were assigned to the work along with their regular duties, the turnover rate was very high, making training and the development of skill almost impossible.[4] The situation in enterprises improved in 1955, but no improvement had taken place in rural areas through 1957. Moreover, statistical services failed to attract young capable people. A national survey in early 1957 revealed that the trainees were "relatively old in age, deficient in memorizing capacity." [5] Contrary to the development in industries and trade, no special educational institution had been established for statistics. It was claimed that "several tens of thousands" had been trained under the program.[6] If so, there were at least 100,000 more in the national statistical working force yet to receive formal training in 1957.

To operate with such a working force gave rise to many problems that had direct bearing on the quality of statistics. At least up to the end of 1955, the morale of the rank and file was very low. For example, in an oil refinery at Fushun (Manchuria), 13 of the 37 statistical workers there were

---

[4] Hsüeh Mu-ch'iao, "Final Report at the Fourth National Statistical Conference," *TCKTTH*, 5: 1–7, May, 1955.

[5] State Statistical Bureau, Department of Education, "Some Problems . . ."

[6] "Record of Director Hsüeh's Report at the Meeting of All Bureau Workers," *TCKT*, 6: 1–6, March, 1957.

found unwilling to stay on the job in 1953. The situation became so general that a national discussion campaign was conducted in the latter half of 1955 to encourage the rank and file to voice their grievances as to why they were unwilling to remain in statistical services. As summarized by the senior deputy director of the State Bureau, the reasons were given in the following order: statistical work was unimportant and without a future; simple adding and subtracting provided no opportunity for demonstrating and developing personal talent; the superiors paid little attention to the work and gave no support when practical difficulties arose; and, finally, the job was too poorly paid.[7]

The consequences of such low morale on statistical work were serious. Statistical materials, state secrets in particular, were lost all the time. Wrong entries, omissions, miscalculations, and fabrications of figures were common. When arbitrary alteration of statistical figures and fictitious reports came to their knowledge, the statistical staff made no effort to expose them or to correct them.[8] In Liaoning province, a survey of the quality of statistics in 232 factories and mines from April to October, 1954 showed that since 1953, according to an incomplete count, 14,300 errors had been made, of which carelessness accounted for 28 per cent, failure to understand the indicators 14 per cent, fictitious reports 3 per cent, deficient statistical organization 27 per cent, defective primary records 18 per cent, and poor management in enterprise 10 per cent.[9] In other words, at least the first three causes, ac-

---

[7] Chia Ch'i-yun, "Conclusions from the Discussion on 'Why Unwilling to Engage in Statistical Work?'" *TCKTTH*, 12: 7–11, December, 1955.

[8] Chia Ch'i-yun, "Study Conscientiously the Resolutions of the Party's Central Committee and Raise the Ideological Level of Statistical Workers," *TCKTTH*, 2: 3–6, May, 1954.

[9] Ma Heng-chih (director of Liaoning Provincial Statistical Bureau), "How to Investigate the Quality of Statistical Figures in Factories and Mines," *TCKTTH*, 3: 10–14, March, 1955.

counting for 45 per cent of the errors, stemmed from the poor quality of statistical personnel. And Liaoning province led the rest of the country in developing statistical services!

In January, 1957, the State Bureau announced that great improvement had been made in the two preceding years not only in statistical work, but in the attitude and operating capacity of the rank and file.[10] Perhaps morale had been improved by raising the pay scale and as a result of the State Bureau's vigorous effort at developing a unified national statistical system with full support from the State Planning Commission. Nevertheless, in view of the nature of the training program, the professional competence of the working force at large was probably confined to not much more than some knowledge in the handling of statistical schedules.

---

[10] Editorial Department, "To our Readers and Authors," *TCKT*, 1: 3–4, January, 1957.

CHAPTER VI

# Summary and Evaluation

From 1949 to 1952 no effort was made to develop a statistical system national in scope. The emphasis in statistical work was placed on the state sector, especially state and joint enterprises, for which a national survey was undertaken as of December, 1949. In agriculture, the land-redistribution program probably resulted in improving the data on cultivated acreage and rural population; for sown area and output, reports were made by the *hsien* governments at their own will. National aggregates for this period were estimates based on a small number of unorganized local surveys, which could not be used for national statistics.

A national statistical system started with the operation of the State Statistical Bureau in October, 1952. Throughout the following five years it received full support from the central authorities of the party and the government, with authority (a) to develop a national organization of its own, (b) to centralize the control over formulation and distribution of statistical schedules, (c) to establish a unified statistical-computation checking system, (d) to centralize the control and supply of basic statistics, and (e) to handle national censuses and sample surveys. How successful the State Bureau had been in attaining these objectives and when success or failure occurred provide an important basis for evaluation of the validity of official statistics published in different years.

In organization, provincial and city statistical bureaus were set up in 1953 and began functioning toward the end of the year. The drive to establish units in all special districts and *hsien* began the following year, and in towns and *hsiang* in 1955 and 1956. Only the effort at the special district level was successful (in 1954). The key to rural areas was the *hsien* where the State Bureau met with virtually complete failure. Thus, throughout the whole period, the entire agricultural sector was served merely by a small number of part-time statistical workers.

The State Bureau did not engage in direct field investigation for data, but relied on the business-affairs system for supply by means of regular schedules. The statistical services in the controlling agencies and enterprises of the system, therefore, were of great importance to the State Bureau. In 1953 it began to assist the controlling agencies in setting up the services, which soon operated well enough in 1954 to enable the State Bureau to prepare and issue in September of that year the first statistical communiqué on the economy. Also in 1953 it started helping state and joint enterprises build up their statistical services. Success came first from the centrally controlled enterprises about September, 1954. It was reported that services had been established in all primary establishments by 1957. Hence, statistical coverage rapidly widened after 1954. However, the keeping of accurate primary records remained a serious problem with all of them.

With regard to private industry and trade, the large-sized enterprises in approximately twenty cities were brought into the regular schedules system in 1953. But reports were found unrealistic and dishonest, nor could they be used to estimate the figures for other private concerns left out of the system. This led to a national survey of individual craftsmen and private industrial enterprises employing more than ten persons in 1954 and to another of private-trade and food-and-drink-catering establishments in 1955. When private industry and trade were completely socialized in 1955–56, the State Bureau began to readjust its records concerning this sector for each year back to 1952. As for agriculture, regular schedules were sent to the provincial governments from 1953 to 1957 with the understanding that the local governments below the provincial level would conduct field investigations before making the returns. After the establishment of statistical units at the special district level in 1954, statistical committees began to be organized in many rural areas for the purpose in 1955. But in reality reports on sown area and output of different crops were made by cadres in the *hsiang* and villages according to their own observation. If investigation was made, the method of model survey was most commonly employed, in which samples were chosen at the will of the investigator, chiefly on the basis of ease of obtaining data. Moreover, reports were invariably readjusted by party and political leaders at every level of local government, where the conflict of interests had to be reconciled between the production bureau which tended to inflate the figures and the bureaus of tax collection and internal trade which tended to do the opposite. Collectivization in 1956 and 1957 did not contribute any improvement to the mechanism of statistical reporting, but rather produced a predominantly upward bias on the part of local leadership in editing the figures. Thus, the agricultural statistics of 1955 were probably the least unsatisfactory for the whole period from 1949 to 1957. Nevertheless, all agricultural statistics were so poor that the director of the State Bureau had to admit at the end of 1957 that such important questions as the size of territorial area and cultivated land remained unanswered.

The State Bureau attempted to exercise quality control through several devices. The unified system of regular schedules, introduced in 1953, embodied the principle of complete count that the State Bureau tried hard to put into effect. The system entailed the development of a set of indicators to be adopted in all schedules with standardized methods of computation and classification. The planning and the central and provincial business-affairs authorities had been consistently using different schedules with diverse definitions and classifications. Difficulties with the planning authorities were not resolved until after the middle of 1955. But, because of their own operational needs, the business-affairs ministries, bureaus, and departments were reluctant to comply. The volume of schedules bore heavily on all primary establishments, and confounded the statistical workers in regard to proper computation and entry. Not only inaccuracy resulted, but the figures so produced could not be used for compiling national statistics. However, the authority of centralizing the formulation and distribution of all schedules could not be effectively enforced by the bureau. Centralization was partly achieved for 1955 and 1956 at the central and provincial levels. In 1957 the business-affairs ministries regained their authority to formulate and distribute their own schedules. In rural areas control was found impossible; the flow of schedules and questionnaires turned into a deluge in 1957. The confusion in statistical schedules was compounded by the difficulties arising from the lack of standardization in weights and measures.

Another device for quality control was the unified statistical-computation checking system that required uniformity in the method of computing national indicators for statistical, financial, and operation records. For uniformity in statistical recording the method of double-channeling of statistical returns was introduced in 1953. It took time for the method to be put into effect. Even in 1954 a large number of state and joint enterprises failed to comply. Since then, however, the scope of application widened. While wide application of this method resulted in some improvement in the quality of statistics, the scheme provided no effective check on recording in primary establishments, and also enabled the controlling agencies to adjust the figures according to their judgment. Uniformity in computation methods for statistical, financial, and operation accounts began in 1956.

Of all the devices for quality control, the one most effectively implemented was unification of statistical figures. From 1949 to 1954 widely discrepant figures were produced and employed by the statistical, planning, and business-affairs agencies on the same level and between different levels of government. None of these figures were recognized as "the authentic" or "the official." To avoid controversy and perhaps also because of the policy in early years to regard statistical figures as state secrets, only percentages were used in public statements. These ratios, however, were so inconsistent and contradictory that observers during this period could not help entertaining grave doubt about the validity of official statistics, raising the question whether there were not two sets of statistics, one fabricated for public consumption and the other corrected for planning. In fact, there were almost as many sets of statistics as data-collecting units in the central and local governments.

In March, 1954, the State Bureau was authorized to reconcile all statistical figures in basic national statistics. This was first achieved in industrial statistics before the end of the year and generally accomplished in the first half of 1955. Thereafter, official statistics began to be published in quantity, perceptibly improved in quality. Unification of statistical figures was also extended to publications, making those figures appearing in newspaper editorials, dispatches, public statements by officials, periodicals and books, as official as those issued by the State Bureau.

Centralizing the supply of basic statistics to the planning authorities—an authority given to the State Bureau also in

March, 1954—was much more difficult, because the planning authorities could obtain data from the business-affairs system more promptly than through the state statistical organization. Only with the full support of the State Planning Commission did the State Bureau attain reasonable success in this centralization in 1955.

Statistical personnel formed the weakest link in the national statistical front. The working force increased from 100,000 in 1953 to nearly 200,000 in 1957. An overwhelming majority of them never had any training in statistics or knowledge in statistical work. Statistical services were not able to recruit young people with ability, most new trainees in 1956 being old in average age, deficient in memorizing power. Morale had been very low among the working force, and only began to improve in 1956. Thus, statistical errors, falsification of data, and fictitious reporting were frequently committed, especially before 1956. It was claimed that the training program, conducted by the state statistical organization and the business-affairs agencies, had given instruction to "several tens of thousands" through 1957. If so, at least one-half of the working force received no formal training, except learning on the job. Moreover, judging from the nature of the program, one may infer that the working force on the whole was equipped with not much  more than some knowledge of filling out statistical schedules.

By putting all these developments together from 1949 to 1957, the year 1954 emerges as the dividing line for the reliability of official statistics. In contrast to the purely internal statistics of the business-affairs system, official statistics (or "national economic statistics" or "basic statistics") are a collection of national indicators, specifically defined to be computed by standardized methods. (They do not cover the military.) Not all percentages currently released before 1954 can properly be regarded as calculations from official statistics. In 1954, however, the state statistical organization was extended from the center practically to its limit, namely, the special districts; statistical services in the business-affairs controlling agencies and in the centrally controlled enterprises began to function; the method of double-channeling of statistical returns started to widen its application; a national census was taken of craftsmen and private industrial enterprises employing more than ten persons. For the first time, the State Bureau was able to issue statistical summaries of the economy. And, the use of telegraphic monthly and quarterly returns became effective in checking the major state and joint enterprises on their implementation of the state plan. It is clear that although established in the late summer of 1952, the State Bureau made its influence felt nationally for the first time in 1954.

The official statistics for the first five years from 1949 to 1953, released in late 1955, are, on the whole, poor estimates, with the exception of the statistics for state and joint industrial enterprises that had varying degrees of reliability. It may be recalled that the first state plan for industrial rehabilitation and construction was based on a national survey of state and joint enterprises of 1949, and the 1952 state economic plan, on the returns from major state and joint enterprises in industry, internal trade, and agriculture. In the first two years of operation, the first five-year plan was in fact a plan of targets in percentages without real data. It was during these two years that the newly established provincial and city statistical bureaus made a concerted effort to search for and collect statistical materials for 1952, the base year of the plan. The base-period figures were finally prepared by the State Bureau in late 1954, although they were physical-output and value-product aggregates without detailed breakdowns.[1]

---

[1] State Statistical Bureau, Department of Industrial Statistics, "Basic Conclusions from Reviewing the Industrial Statistical Work of 1954,

From 1954 onward, however, the quality of official statistics improved and statistical coverage broadened. In 1955, definitions, classifications, and computing methods regarding national indicators were made uniform between statistics and planning. More important was the unification of statistical figures between the state statistical organization and the business-affairs system, producing "final" figures for each year back to 1952. Even in agriculture, as has been said, some semblance of control was installed for the first time in the form of statistical committees; and the first of a series of national surveys of family budgets and of agricultural producers' coöperatives was initiated. It was also in 1955 that the State Bureau began to "compute" national income instead of "making a preliminary estimate" as in 1953. In 1956, primary records of erstwhile private industry and trade were made available for the first time to the state statistical organization, so that the early official statistics might be properly adjusted. Clearly it was due to the increased reliability of data and the widening of statistical coverage that the work program of the state statistical services for 1956 and 1957 called for processing all statistical materials for important indicators since 1949 as well as those of 1936 in order to make them comparable year to year and also comparable to those of other people's democracies.

Needless to say, such gradual improvement in reliability and accuracy was only relative. The quality of statistics varies greatly from field to field. In early 1955, the director of the State Bureau gave a relatively objective analysis of comparative reliability as follows: (a) in terms of functional fields, industry was fair; trade, worse; agriculture, worst; (b) in terms of sectors, the state sector was fair; the capitalist sector,

and the Work Program for 1955," *TCKTTH*, 9: 1–7, December, 1954; and "Record of Director Hsüeh's Report at the Meeting of All Bureau Workers," *TCKT*, 6: 1–6, March, 1957.

worse; and the individual sector (craftsmen and family agriculture), worst; (c) in the state sector, the locally controlled
enterprises were worse than those centrally controlled; and
nonbasic activities (such as industrial statistics of nonindustry
ministries, trade statistics of nontrade ministries) were much
worse than basic activities; and (d) in terms of indicators,
physical output and value-product were fair; labor and wages,
worse; finance and cost, worst.[2] At the end of 1955, the State
Bureau in an editorial commented further on the relative
quality of different functional statistics by dividing them into
two groups according to the strength of their foundation. The
first group, having a fair foundation, included, in a *decreasing*
order of strength: industry, transportation and communication, trade, and basic construction. In industry, better than
others were the statistics of state enterprises, which, however, were confined to those for value-product, physical-output, and labor force; statistics for such indicators as trial-
manufacturing, output quota, and utilization of equipment
had not been satisfactorily computed, if at all. The second
group, having a weak foundation, comprised, in an *increasing*
order of weakness, material allocation, culture, education and
health, population, finance and cost, labor and wages, and
agriculture. In agricultural statistics, the weakest were those
on sown area, cultivated acreage, and production, by crops,
according to economic classes; on size and production of livestock; and so on.[3] Complete socialization of private enterprises and agriculture in 1956 and 1957 does not affect these
conclusions on the relative reliability of different types of
statistics.

[2] Hsüeh Mu-ch'iao, "Final Report at the Fourth National Statistical
Conference," *TCKTTH*, 5: 1–7, May, 1955. Most probably, the state
sector was meant to include joint enterprises.
[3] Editorial, "The Need to Perform Statistical Services Diligently, Fast,
Well, and Economically in order to Meet National Construction Needs,"
*TCKTTH*, 2: 3–6, January, 1956.

In spite of all the State Bureau's effort at building up a state statistical system since 1952, yet the bureau rated the best type of statistics merely as "fair." Why is it that none could be rated as "good"? The answer clearly lies in such factors as low quality of the statistical working force, disorderliness in primary records, poor management in enterprises, confusion in the weights-and-measures system, and lack of standardization equipment. All these will take time to improve and, indeed, are none other than a manifestation of underdevelopment of the country.

Part Two: The Disaster

CHAPTER VII

# Decentralization, the Great Leap and Statistical Services

## DECENTRALIZATION AND THE GREAT LEAP

Great strides had been taken during the period of the first five-year plan in the establishment of a state statistical system, with the State Statistical Bureau operating a national network of services at the provincial and the special-district levels, exercising centralized control over the quality and supply of basic national statistics. Great opposition was encountered on the way, especially from the business-affairs ministries and departments; but the bureau had always been able to secure full backing from the center. Confident of the continuation of this support, the director of the bureau mapped out, at the Sixth National Statistical Conference held at Peiping in September, 1957, a work program for the second five-year period (1958–1962) that listed as high-priority items the institution of regular services at the *hsien,* district, and *hsiang* levels, the improvement of services in the primary establishments, and the gradual introduction of services in the agricultural collectives.[1]

At the time of this conference, however, Peiping was already drafting the plan of decentralizing control over public finance and industrial and commercial enterprises that was to take effect at the beginning of 1958. Under the plan more than 80 per cent of the centrally controlled enterprises were to be

---

[1] "Director Hsüeh's Report at the Sixth National Statistical Conference," *TCKT,* 21: 1–21, November, 1957.

transferred to provincial jurisdiction. Nevertheless, according
to his final report to the conference, Director Hsüeh did not
anticipate that such a sweeping reorganization in the administrative machinery of the country would have any effect on
the state statistical system, other than enhancing the importance of the provincial statistical bureaus as direct sources of
data for the State Bureau.[2] Little was it realized, then, that
decentralization would presently reinforce the "great leap
forward" movement which in turn would shatter the whole
system to its foundation.

It seems that the great leap as a national movement started
first in agriculture toward the end of October, 1957, and spread
rapidly to industry and trade soon after the decentralization
program was put into effect on January 1, 1958.[3] The movement in agriculture was centrally planned and directed,
requiring mass mobilization in the rural areas for capital
construction projects, leading to the introduction of common
mess halls and the development of people's communes. In
contrast, the large advance in industrial output and in basic
investment during the first few months of 1958 was unplanned
and unexpected—the result of unleashing local initiative under
decentralization. As Director Hsüeh of the State Bureau
observed in June, 1958,

The growth rate of factory value product during the second five-
year plan was at first thought to be lower than that of the first
five years (19.2 per cent annually), but now after decentralization
the average annual rate of increase is likely to be at least over 20
per cent and may even be over 30 per cent.[4]

[2] It will be recalled that statistical reports of all locally controlled
enterprises reach the State Bureau only through the provincial bureaus.
See the discussion on the "double-tracked system" on pp. 41–42, above.

[3] See my "Economic Development," *The China Quarterly*, 1: 35–50,
January-March, 1960; especially 42–44.

[4] "Record of Director Hsüeh's Remarks at the Statistical Meeting in
Honan Province," *TCKT*, 12: 1–4, June, 1958. See also Chia Fu, "On
the Growth Rate of the National Economy during the Period of the
Second Five-Year Plan," *CHCC*, 10: 4–7, October, 1956.

The great leap is a movement in which the people are exhorted to make all effort humanly possible to advance on all economic and cultural fronts—the production front in particular. The mechanism by which the movement runs consists of an endless chain of emulative drives among workers, factories, agricultural collectives, production teams, and localities.

Nationally, even for any one objective, the quota for the year may undergo continuous upward revision by the central party authorities, as happened in 1958. The central authorities used to determine, according to the principle of balance, one single set of national targets which the provinces together were expected to reach or overreach during the year. Now this way of applying the principle of balance was severely criticised as an expression of "conservatism," involving the errors of regarding the balance as "passive," "static," and "absolute," and of "detachment from the masses," that is, ignoring what the masses could do with whipped-up enthusiasm.[5] These errors were to be rectified, partly through decentralization that had already started, and partly through adopting "the system of planning with two accounts." Under this system two sets of targets would be used instead of one at every level of government. In the hands of the central government were to be not only the "first" set of quotas which it had determined and which each province would guarantee to fulfill, but also the "second" set of targets above and beyond the level set forth in the first set that represented what each province after internal discussion was reasonably sure to reach. This "second" set for the central government was, in turn, to be the "first" set for the provincial government in the sense that the cities and *hsien* under its control would have

---

[5] Yang Ying-chieh, "The Principle of Balance in Planning for the National Economy," *HH*, 12: 26–27, June, 1958; and Ch'eng Chenchia, "A Great Leap in Planning under the Anti-Waste and Anti-Conservatism Movement," *CHCC*, 4: 5–6, April, 1958.

to guarantee attainment of the targets specified therein. Again, like the central government, each provincial government had also its own "second" set of targets that the cities and *hsien* felt confident they could achieve. By the same token, there were also two sets of targets for each *hsien* government in its relation with the towns, *hsiang*, and villages.[6] As a result, a national quota would automatically become bigger in the successively lower levels of local government. And when the national quota itself continued to be revised upward in line with the glowing reports from the field, local targets had to be raised *pari passu*, which, in turn, would induce a further upward revision of the national goal. Thus, the nature of the planning mechanism inevitably generated a great leap—in targets. As one of the members of the State Planning Commission truthfully said, "the method of planning with two accounts is an innovation not only in China but also in all socialist countries." [7]

While some objectives of emulation are national in scope (like steel production by backyard furnaces), many others are of necessity local, decided upon from time to time by local party and government leaders. Whatever the objective may be at the time in a community, the drive is identified as the "focal-point program," for which all relevant statistics, especially those showing daily or weekly progress (known as "progress statistics"), are indispensable to the leadership both for policy-making and for stimulating the workers and peasants to further exertion. For the first time statistics take on great local importance, serving a purpose that calls for types of data, methods of computation, and timing of presentation—all different from those required in basic national

---

[6] Liao Chi-li, "About the Two-Account System, *CHCC*, 5: 8–9, May, 1958; and, Wei I, "Revolution in the Method of Planning," *HH*, 8: 10–12, April, 1958.

[7] Liao, *op. cit.*

statistics. Thus, the great leap brought the local party and political leaders in direct conflict with the state statistical authorities regarding the operation of the whole statistical system.

## The Shattering Effect on the System

Criticism was focused on the centralization of operational authority over the entire state statistical service in the hands of the State Bureau, on the ground that this had made the service "detached from politics and from reality." [8] The charge of "unreality" was based mainly on the observation that the regular statistical schedules had nothing to do with the focal-point programs. The formulation of these schedules—from the selection of indicators to the format of tables—was determined by the State Bureau according to its own needs. Local party and government authorities, while having complete control over local economic and political affairs, were not permitted, without prior approval from the bureau, to modify the schedules according to their needs or to issue new schedules. The same was true of the schedules used within a business-affairs ministerial hierarchy. Such a divorce from reality gave rise to the much more serious charge of "detachment from politics." It was said that with the bureau placing so much emphasis on the national work program to the exclusion of local needs, all local statistical offices, although organizationally part of the local governments, tended "to ignore local party and political leadership." [9]

These faults were now held to have been responsible also for the lack of development of statistical services in rural

---

[8] T'ao Yen (deputy director of the State Bureau), "Report at the Wuhan Meeting of Statistical Workers," *TCYC*, 5: 4–8, May, 1958.

[9] Chia Ch'i-yun, "Several Problems in the present Reform Movement of Statistical Services," *TCKT*, 15: 5–10, August, 1958.

areas. Take Hopei province, for instance, where state statistical units had been organized down to the *hsien* level as early as 1953 but no further as late as 1957.[10] These units regarded as their whole assignment the program set up by the bureau, which was not more than the reporting, in the course of a year, of three sown areas (spring, summer, and fall) and two harvests (summer and fall), *plus* one or two special economic surveys. This work could not keep the personnel occupied throughout the year. Moreover, the materials so collected did not meet the operational needs of the local party and government authorities, who required daily or weekly reports on a wide variety of economic activities that were supervised directly by the "production office" and other operational units of the local government. Since the state statistical personnel were not fully occupied and their work was not directly relevant, they were often coöpted for other assignments unrelated to statistical work. Meanwhile, the staff of the production office and other related units found themselves devoting increasingly more of their time to collecting various statistical information from the agricultural collectives and *hsiang*. And the cadres at these primary levels, not used to statistical work and unable to cope with the flood of questionnaires and statistical forms coming from above, were driven to submitting "false estimates and false reports." [11] It is, therefore, not surprising that the state statistical services had not been placed on a going basis at the *hsien* level, let alone the levels below, and that the public had long been regarding all rural statistics as "30 per cent fabrication and 70 per cent

---

[10] Hu Kai-ming, "Remarks at the National Statistical Meeting (Paoting, Hopei province)," *TCKT*, 13: 3–6, July, 1958; and *JMJP*, April 29, 1958.

[11] "Depend on the Masses for Setting up Statistical Services in the *Hsien, Hsiang,* and Agricultural Collectives," *JMJP*, April 29, 1958.

guesswork." [12] Apparently, this whole description was applicable to other provinces as well.[13]

Amid this nation-wide criticism of the state statistical service, the bureau director—the architect of the system from its inception—at first was only willing to concede that the statistical personnel should allocate some of their time to collect progress statistics for the local party and government authorities. In early April, 1958, he spoke publicly to his working force in these terms:

Since the establishment of the State Statistical Bureau, statistical schedules have multiplied so much that their designing and compiling alone engage more than 80 per cent of the efforts of the central and provincial bureaus. Henceforth, the central bureau should consider devoting one-third of its time to the schedules, one-third to investigations required by the party and the government, and the remaining one-third to statistical analysis. The provincial bureaus should engage themselves more than before in economic surveys and analysis. As to the units at the *hsien* level, 90 per cent of their time should be used for collecting progress statistics in connection with the focal-point program of the locality, and 10 per cent for compiling the regular statistics on three sown areas and two harvests.[14]

Obviously, in this reorientation Director Hsüeh was attempting to ward off any encroachment on the operational independence and integrity of the state statistical service. In fact, when writing for the Soviet journal of statistics about this time, he stated that the first lesson derived from experience in the

---

[12] Li Chi-p'ing, "How has the Party Directed and Utilized Statistical Services?" *TCKT*, 13: 7–13, July, 1958.

[13] See, for example, the situation in Honan province, as reported by Teng I-chuan (director of the provincial bureau of Honan), "Excerpt of Teng's Remarks at the Joint Meeting of Party Secretaries and Statistical-Unit Chiefs of the *Hsien* Level," *TCKT*, 12: 5–8, June, 1958.

[14] Hsüeh Mu-ch'iao, "To Establish a Unified Control System of Agricultural Statistical Service is the Road to Develop Statistical Work in the *Hsien*," *TCKT*, 8: 1–4, April, 1958.

development of statistical services in China was that "statistical work should serve the purpose of socialist construction and be closely related to the planning administration of the national economy." [15] The implication is clearly that statistical work should not be subject to local control.

But to readjust the work program in terms of local needs met only part of the critics' demands, for the charge of "detachment from politics and from reality" was soon broadened to bring under fire most of the basic principles under which the statistical system had been operating from the beginning.[16] For example, the critics objected to the state service making use of statistics to check on the performance of enterprises which were now relegated to local control. Of much greater significance was the opposition to unified computing methods and statistical methodology. The rule that all computation methods must be formulated by the bureau for the country as a whole was attacked as a case of "dogmatism," on the ground that it failed to take into account the wide diversity of local conditions.[17] The implication concerning national statistics was obviously not appreciated by the critics. Equally pointedly, the bureau was taken to task for giving too much weight to the principle of complete coverage and statistical methodology, therefore ignoring the importance of model surveys that were supposed to have been first introduced by Mao Tse-tung in his early agrarian investigations in Hunan

---

[15] "Statistical Work in the People's Republic of China," *Vestnik Statistiki* [Statistical Herald], 7: 20–24, July, 1958. In this article, Hsüeh pointed out altogether three lessons from the experience, the other two being that (1) statistical work in a socialist country should utilize fully the advantages of a socialist economy in developing statistics of all kinds, and (2) for the purpose of planning it is necessary to establish recording in all enterprises and organizations so that all aspects of economic activity may be comprehensively and continuously observed.

[16] For these basic principles, see pp. 14–15, above.

[17] Chao I-wen, "My Recognition of Dogmatism in Statistical Services," *TCYC*, 5: 9–12, May, 1958.

province.[18] The force of the attack must have been particularly strong, for Director Hsüeh, the chief sponsor of the complete-enumeration principle, was compelled to make this admission at the statistical meeting of Honan province in June, 1958:

In the past some people have held that statistics do not admit of estimation. After these years of service I have come to reverse my position. . . . To combine estimates with statistics is the real ability of a statistician. . . . With 10 per cent or 1 per cent of data he may compute the universe accurately. . . . In regard to cotton yarn and cotton cloth statistics 99 per cent accuracy was achieved [by estimation]; but less than 99 per cent accuracy [was achieved] in the case of agricultural output.[19]

Significantly, Hsüeh made no reference to the need of restraints in the use of estimates for statistical purposes.

That the whole system was under attack was made even clearer by one of the deputy directors of the bureau who was destined to succeed to the directorship in about a year: "In the last few years so much emphasis has been given to nation-wide unification of the various measures of the statistical system that they are bound to be rigid, mechanical and at variance with local conditions." [20] With such an admission from the state statistical authorities, a radical reorganization of the service was inevitable. It was initiated early in July, 1958, when Hsüeh convened what was probably the last national statistical conference at Paoting, Hopei province.[21] At this

---

[18] T'ao Yen, *op. cit.* For the principle of complete coverage, see also p. 37, above.

[19] *TCKT*, 12: 1–4, June, 1958.

[20] Chia Ch'i-yun, *op. cit.*

[21] A national statistical conference differs from a conference of provincial and city bureau directors in that it includes in its membership also the chiefs of statistical divisions in the business-affairs system and in the local governments of various levels. The conference held in July, 1958, should have been called the Eighth National Conference, but the fact that it was not so labeled might indicate that the State Bureau no longer expected to exercise direct operational control over all these units. Since then, only conferences of provincial and city bureau directors have been held.

conference Hsüeh appealed to the rank and file "to fight bitterly for three months so as to make a great leap in statistical work." [22] This was the battle cry of the so-called "national statistical work-reform movement." Allegedly, the reform was virtually accomplished by October 1, 1958.[23]

The reform included two major moves. One was integration of the statistical work program into emulative drives taking place at various levels of government. The state statistical service was required to provide the appropriate party and government leaders with the following types of data: "background statistics" for the drive during the planning stage; "progress statistics" to check on implementation during the drive (quarterly for the central government, monthly for provincial governments, and many more for *hsien* governments and below); and "comparative statistics" to stimulate competition among groups, operational units (like factories) and localities.[24] Local needs were thus given priority over the work on national statistics. Like those engaged in statistical work in rural areas, the statistical personnel in various enterprises were advised to spend not more than 10 per cent of their time and effort to do the work assigned to them by the statistical unit above, the other 90 per cent to be used in meeting the statistical needs of the enterprise. It was reported that by the beginning of October, 1958, statistical units everywhere—from rural to urban areas, from primary levels to provinces, from industrial and agricultural production to basic construction, trade, culture, and health—were already deeply engaged in progress statistics in connection with focal-point programs. The extent of reorganization varied: in many prov-

---

[22] "Director Hsüeh's Concluding Report at the National Statistical Conference at Paoting," *TCKT*, 14: 2–8, July, 1958; also, *TCYC*, 7: 1–4, July, 1958.

[23] Editorial, "The National Statistical Work Reform is Basically Completed," *TCKT*, 19: 6–8, October, 1958.

[24] In 1958, monthly telegraphic reports on implementation and progress to the State Bureau were introduced.

inces, the state statistical services took care of only the essential parts of progress statistics, leaving the rest, as before, to the business-affairs departments; in some other provinces, all statistical personnel of different departments at the *hsien* level were centralized into one unit, to be in charge of both comprehensive and progress statistics; and finally, in some small areas, the existing state statistical unit took over all statistical services which used to be performed by many other units. It was further reported that generally the statistical personnel had become so adept in producing progress statistics that the data could be gathered within 5 to 10 hours at the *hsien* level, within 10 to 24 hours at the special-district level, and within 10 to 30 hours at the provincial level; and that it would take 3 days at the most to compile statistics for a whole province.[25]

The other major reform was based on the policy of "operating the statistical services by the whole party and all the people," that is, mass participation in statistical work under party leadership. Mass participation was considered essential, partly because the supply of reliable data depended upon full coöperation of the masses—especially data on agriculture and on industrial production by indigenous methods which became increasingly important under the great leap forward;[26] and partly because the public's confidence in the progress statistics used in emulative drives would be enhanced if the contestants were allowed to question the truthfulness of the figures.[27] Local party leadership meant complete domination over organization and operation by party secretaries at various levels. The development in Hopei province, though far ahead of other provinces, furnishes an illustration. There the statistical services in rural areas were completely reorganized in March, 1958. In the *hsien* government a statis-

[25] Editorial as cited in note 23.
[26] "An Account of the National Conference of Provincial Statistical Bureau Directors," *TCKT*, 21: 1–3, November, 1958.
[27] Li Chi-p'ing, *op. cit.*

tical unit for the whole "county" was established, with the
*hsien* party secretary as chairman and the *hsien* magistrate as
his deputy; likewise, the unit at the district level was headed
by the district party secretary. At the *hsiang* level was the
statistical station, headed jointly by a local party secretary
and the *hsiang* chief, with the *hsiang* party branch secretary
as their deputy, and the chief accountants of the agricultural
collectives as members. Finally, in each collective a statistical
committee was established, headed by the party branch secretary and the chief of the collective, with the chief accountant
as their deputy, and the recorders of various production
teams as members.[28] Apparently, within the next few
months the same reorganization took place in the rural areas
of many other provinces, for the reform has since been identified as the Great Reform Movement of Rural Statistical Work
of 1958.[29]

At the provincial and city levels where the state statistical
network had been well entrenched, the local party authorities
did not attempt to reorganize the local statistical bureau in
the same way as they did in rural areas, but their domination
over the operations was no less pervasive. Taking again Hopei
province as a case in point, beginning in July, 1958, all statistical offices at the provincial and other local levels below
were required to submit to the party committee of the same
level for final approval all statistical schedules, statistical
indicators, reporting dates, and computing methods that had
been demanded of them in the state statistical hierarchy.
Should the local party committee have a different opinion on
any of these matters, the statistical unit at the next higher level
would either respect such a judgment and approve the cor-

---

[28] *Ibid.*
[29] Editorial, "The Necessity of Bringing about an All-Front Leap in
Rural Statistical Work," *CHYTC*, 2: 4–6, February, 1960.

responding change; or request the party committee to recon-
sider, taking all the factors in the local and national situation
into account, or, as a final resort, appeal to the party committee
on its own level. As for computation methods, those prescribed
by the higher statistical authorities should be followed; those
not so prescribed might be devised by the office or unit locally;
and finally those that had been prescribed but were found at
variance with local conditions might be modified by the units
at the levels of special district, city, or *hsien*.[30]

The national statistical work reform was soon carried to its
logical limit in many provinces and localities—by raising the
issue of whether there was any need for a specialized statistical service at all. Since statistical services were to be performed under local party leadership and direction, was there
any longer a need for an independent state statistical network?
Since each of the business-affairs departments had been maintaining its own statistical services for operational and planning purposes, why should there be a separate statistical office
at the same local level? As a result, statistical units were
abolished or their statistical personnel was heavily reduced
in many areas, leaving the work to be done by the business-
affairs departments.[31] In fact, since "statistical services are
to be performed by the party and the masses," the very con-
cept that statistical work is so specialized as to require a
separate unit with a trained working force was no longer
valid even within a business-affairs department or within an
enterprise. Thus, in many a business-affairs hierarchy such as
the Ministry of Transportation, statistical units were either
dissolved or merged with other units in some areas, and in

[30] Yuen Po, "On the Direction of Statistical Work," *TCYC*, 7: 5–8,
July, 1958.
[31] Chia Ch'i-yun, "On the Problems of Policy concerning China's Statistical Work," *CHYTC*, 10: 1–6, July, 1959.

many other areas the staff were regularly detailed to work
in other focal-point programs.[32] At the end of 1958 both the
state statistical system and the services in the business-affairs
system were gradually going out of existence.

[32] Kung Chang-chen, "The present Tasks in Transportation Statistics," *CHYTC*, 11: 4–5, August, 1959.

# CHAPTER VIII

# The Statistical Fiasco of 1958

The developments in 1958, especially those regarding the so-called national statistical work reform, dealt a severe blow to those who had devoted themselves to building up the state statistical system since 1952. Every one of the guiding principles for the development of the system was being discredited, if not discarded. Whereas the system focused its attention on gathering data that were homogeneous and reasonably accurate for the purpose of compiling national statistics, the prevailing practice shifted the emphasis to local needs, mostly statistics that would boost local emulative drives. Such local services were given top priority, claiming as much as 90 per cent of the statistical personnel's time in primary establishments and at primary government levels. It is true that the agricultural statistical work reform, as part of the national reform, did improve on the State Bureau's performance by extending the statistical network to most of the *hsien* and the levels below; but all the new units as well as the old operated at these levels under the personal direction of local party secretaries, and no longer as part of the state statistical hierarchy. In training, perhaps partly because of this sudden expansion of services, mass participation through "political education" was developed at the expense of improving the technical competence of the existing working force and the new recruits. Even the professional nature of statistical work was denied. The trend had already started to eliminate "statistical" units and personnel at various government levels and in enterprises. Under these circumstances, it is to be expected that national statistics, those for agriculture in particular, would suffer. In 1958 the result turned out to be a fiasco.

The main facts are familiar. The incredible claims for the accomplishments of the great leap, issued from time to time throughout 1958 and in the early months of 1959, finally culminated in Premier Chou's announcement in April, 1959, that the output of food grains and raw cotton had each increased about 102.5 per cent from 1957 to 1958 and that the plan for 1959 called for a continuous great leap in the output of food grains by 40 per cent and of raw cotton by 50 per cent. The specter of hunger was thus exorcised forever from the Chinese scene. Within four months, however, the government formally admitted exaggeration, the claims for the 1958 output of the two items being scaled down by about one-third and the targets for their output in 1959 decreased by about one-half. There were also downward revisions of the output data for several other crops.

For any statistical service this is a disaster of the first magnitude. Not only the reliability of the revised data but the validity of all Peiping statistics were thus open to serious question. It is, therefore, important to go into details as to what had actually occurred in agricultural and industrial statistics.

AGRICULTURAL STATISTICS

We have seen that the great leap movement needs statistics in relation to the focal-point programs. In particular, progress statistics are needed most, to be used for publicity and for stimulating the people to further effort. Lest the people should feel discouraged at their own exertion, it is only natural that the figures are generally made to show a direct correlation between effort and output. Moreover, having designed and activated the focal-point programs that demand the concerted effort of the community, the local authorities cannot afford to admit of anything but fulfillment or overfulfillment of the quota. This is especially true of the cadres in the field responsible for carrying out the program among the masses. In either case, to admit failure is to invite the serious charge of "rightist-conservatism," the lack of faith in the efficacy of the great leap or any other basic policy of the party. As a result, the cadres and local authorities in 1958 were driven to fabricating glowing reports on accomplishments; or, in some instances, the cadres prepared two sets of figures, one higher than the other, which were at the disposal of the authorities.[1] Finally, when interlocality emulations are held, as they frequently were in 1958, the inflating of claims by one place tends to be both the cause and effect of inflating by another.[2] In short, as tools of strategy for emulative drives, all progress statistics are inherently upwardly biased, if not purely fictional.

Thus the extent of deliberate falsification in progress statistics depends on the pressure to reach a target. However, there were three special circumstances that made the progress statistics of agricultural output in 1958 run all the wilder, namely, the continuous upward revision of goals for agriculture, the wide application of the method of "model survey," and the disruption of the people's commune movement. Toward the end of 1958, all measures for agricultural development were conveniently brought together under the so-called "eight-word charter," the words being "soil" (deep ploughing), "fertilizer" (accumulation), "water" (conservation), "seed" (selection), "denseness" (in cropping), "protection" (from pests), "implement" (improvement), and "farm" (management). For many

---

[1] Wei Heng (governor and party secretary of Shansi province), "Develop the Practice of Verification and Establish Accurate Statistical Services," *CHYTC*, 6: 1–3, March, 1959. See also p. 46, above.

[2] For "dishonesty" and "fabrication" practices in regard to 1958 statistics, see editorial, "Develop the Practice of Verification," *CHYTC*, 2: 1–2, January, 1959.

years these measures had been variously practiced or tried out in different localities and regions; in 1958 they were given uniform emphasis throughout the country. During the year, in the *hsien* and the levels below in each province, virtually every focal-point program was framed in terms of these measures according to the stage of the agricultural season; for example, the focal point might be fertilizer collection, area sown, deep ploughing, close cropping, amount harvested, and so on. The cadres as well as the peasantry were told with finality that adoption of these measures would result in increasing output manifold, as had been conclusively proved in experimental stations or certain farms, provided only that proper leadership on the part of the cadres was forthcoming. In fact, local production quotas were determined in the national plan on the basis of the expected results. Hence, local cadres and authorities were pressured into reporting accomplishments in line with or above the planned quota. But when these extravagant claims were reported to Peiping, the central authorities—and this is characteristic of 1958—kept revising upward the national goal for the year (see table 2 below), which in turn prodded the cadres to inflate their claims further. As the final target called for a doubling of grain output above the level of 185 million tons in 1957, unsurprisingly national statistics did record a harvest of 375 million tons for 1958.

Such inflated claims were possible in 1958 because the statistical services in the countryside were operationally as well as organizationally independent of the state statistical system. All methods of investigation hitherto prescribed by the State Bureau were generally discarded as inconsistent with local needs, which required that progress statistics be compiled within a matter of hours. The method that meets this requirement is model survey. It will be recalled that the method allows the investigator to choose, at his own will, one or several objects of investigation as typical of the universe.[3] To obtain a figure of any desirable magnitude requires not more than choosing as the model a farm with above-average unit-area productivity, and multiplying its yield by the total cropped area of a *hsiang* or a district; the result may be honestly said to have been founded on field investigation. That the use of this method was chiefly responsible for the exaggerated claims was asserted by the State Bureau in its announcement of correction of the 1958 data: "Lacking the experience of estimating the output of such an uprecedented bumper crop [as 1958], the agricultural statistical offices have overestimated them in most cases."[4] Had the bureau been in a position to insist on complete enumeration, a large margin of error might yet have been present in the reports, but such fantastic claims as those of 1958 would have been checked with relative ease. As if to furnish proof that the method of model survey was officially held responsible for the gross inaccuracies of 1958 statistics, the director of research in the State Bureau, beginning January, 1959, published in the official journal a series of five articles on the way in which model surveys should be conducted.[5]

The disruption of whatever the existing regular statistical services in the countryside by the rise of people's communes in the latter part of 1958 must also be identified as another reason for the fiasco. The organization of the communes began taking on the character of nation-wide mobilization in August, 1958 before the fall harvest. Within forty-five days, as it was

[3] See above, p. 30.
[4] State Statistical Bureau, "Communiqué on Correction of the 1958 Agricultural Statistics," *JMJP*, August 27, 1959.
[5] Yang Po, "How to Conduct Model Surveys," *CHYTC*, 1: 36–37; 2: 36–37; 3: 24–25; 4: 40–41; and 5: 36–37, January to March, 1959. See also Chen Ying-chung, "A Wider Application of the Method of Model Survey," *ibid.*, 6: 34–36, March, 1959.

reported, 121,936,350 households, representing 98 per cent of all rural households, had been organized into 26,425 people's communes.[6] Since the communes in general did not begin to establish statistical units of their own until the spring of 1959, the *hsien* government continued to rely on the reporting services in the former districts, *hsiang*, and collectives. These services, mostly established during the rural statistical-work reform, were severely disrupted by the sweeping rural reorganization. Even if local party authorities, who were now in full charge of statistical services, were capable of a satisfactory job, they would be unable, because of their preoccupation with the commune movement, to check adequately—if their checking were ever of any value—the statistical reports prepared by the more or less regular reporting staff. Indeed, since most of the latter were either cadres or activists, devoting only a small part of their time to statistical work, they were not likely to have time for reporting during the first few busy months of the commune movement. Invariably, reporting on the autumn harvests and preparation of the annual returns were very much left to those totally uninitiated in this type of work.

Under these circumstances, what were the original claims for the agricultural output of 1958? How different were they from the figures announced by the State Bureau in April, 1959? If the original claims had already been scaled down by the bureau in April, what occurred in the ensuing four months that prompted another drastic revision? Answers to these questions, on which a proper evaluation of national statistics since 1957 depends, may best be sought by comparing the development of targets and finalized output figures

---

[6] "Virtually all Agricultural Villages in China have been Communized," *TCKT*, 20: 23, October, 1958; also State Statistical Bureau, *Wei-ta ti shih-nien* [The Great Ten Years], Peiping, September, 1959, p. 36.

for each year from 1957 to 1960. Table 2 below requires extended analysis.

For 1957 the following observations may be made. First, although the plan for any particular year has to be submitted to and approved by the National People's Congress that meets during the year, it may or may not be the same as the plan that had already been put into effect at the beginning of the year. During the interval the targets may be raised or lowered, depending on prospects; they were reduced in 1957, but were raised considerably in 1958. Second, estimates are usually released at the end of the year or in January of the following year, not only for the sake of giving publicity to the achievements, but, more importantly, as the basis for determining the targets for the current year. Just as the 1957 plan published in February of the year was based on the estimates of the 1956 performance (not shown in the table), so the 1958 plan published in February of that year rested on the estimated results for the previous year. Third, the finalized statistics for 1957, not released by the State Bureau in its annual communiqué until April, 1959, were already made public in book form by the Ministry of Agriculture in October, 1958 (presumably with the knowledge and approval of the bureau). The ministry, through its Bureau of Planning, was then the agency that collected and prepared national statistics on agriculture. Apparently it had won the battle over the State Bureau as to who should do this work.[7] Finally, the estimated figures and the finalized statistics were identical for such major items as food grain and raw cotton, and were virtually the same even for the subgroups of food grains. However, this was not true for other items; in some instances the adjustment in the finalized statistics was quite substantial, either upward or downward. It is remarkable that despite

---

[7] See above, pp. 33–34.

Table 2. Selected Agricultural Statistics, 1957–1960

| Item | Unit | 1957 | | | | 1958 | | | | | 1959 | | 1960 | |
|---|---|---|---|---|---|---|---|---|---|---|---|---|---|---|
| | | Plan 2/57[1] | Plan 7/57[2] | Estimated 2/58[3] | Final 10/58[4] | Plan 2/58[5] | Early leap target | Estimate 1/59[5] | Final 4/59[6] | Revised 8/59[7] | Plan 4/58[8] | Plan 8/59[9] | Final 3/60[8] | Plan 3/60[10] |
| | | (1) | (2) | (3) | (4) | (5) | (6) | (7) | (8) | (9) | (10) | (11) | (12) | (13) |
| Food grains | Million tons | 197.5 | 191 | 185.00 | 185.00 | 196.00 | 212.5[11] | 375.0[12] | 375 | 250.0 | 525 | 275.0 | 270.0 | 297.0 |
| rice | Million tons | | | 86.50[13] | 86.80 | | 180.0[14] | 160.0 | | 118.7 | | | | |
| wheat | Million tons | | | 23.50[13] | 23.60 | | 52.0[15] | 40.0 | | 29.0 | | | | |
| potatoes[a] | Million tons | | | 21.40[13] | 21.90 | | 105.0[16] | 92.2 | | 45.4 | | | | |
| coarse | Million tons | | | 53.50[13] | 52.70 | | | 92.4 | | 61.9 | | | | |
| Ginned cotton | Thousand tons | 1,650.0 | 1,500 | 1,640.00 | 1,640.00 | 1,750.00 | 1,975.0[11] | 3,350.0 | 3,319 | 2,100.0 | 5,000 | 2,310.0 | 2,410.0 | 2,650.0 |
| Soy beans | Thousand tons | 10,550.0 | | 9,950.00[17] | 10,045.00 | 10,400.00 | | 12,500.0 | 12,500 | 10,500.0 | 15,000 | | 11,500.0 | |
| Groundnuts | Thousand tons | | | 2,870.00[18] | 2,571.00 | 3,445.00 | | 6,300.0 | 4,000 | 2,800.0 | 6,000 | 3,000.0[19] | | |
| Tobacco, cured | Thousand tons | | | 293.00[18] | 256.00 | 434.00[18] | | 700.0 | | 380.0 | 1,000[20] | 250.0[19] | | |
| Jute and hemp | Thousand tons | | | 309.00 | 313.00 | | | 375.0[21] | 325[8] | 320[22] | 500 | | | |
| Rapeseed | Thousand tons | | | 910.00 | 888.00 | 1,180.00 | | 1,385.0 | 1,100[8] | 1,100.0 | 1,600 | | | |
| Sugar cane | Thousand tons | | | 10,201.00 | 10,392.00 | 13,033.00 | | 20,000.0[21] | 13,525[8] | 13,525.0 | 20,000 | | | |
| Sugar beets | Thousand tons | | | 1,840.00 | 1,501.00 | 2,394.00 | | 3,000.0[21] | 2,900[8] | 2,900.0 | 5,500 | | | |
| Pigs | Million head | 120.0 | 110 | 127.80[18] | 145.90 | 150.00[24] | | 200.0 | 180[8] | 160.0 | 280 | 180.0 | | 243.0 |
| Afforested area | Million ha. | | 3 | 3.00 | 4.40[22] | | 33.0[25] | 30.0 | | 17.5 | 40[26] | | 36.0[27] | 49.3 |
| Agricultural-value product at 1957 prices[b] | Billion yuan | | | | 53.70[7] | | | | 88[28] | 67.1 | 122[28] | 73.8 | 78.3 | 88.0 |
| Over-all agricultural-value product[b] at 1957 prices | Billion yuan | | | 64.87 | | 68.83 | | | | | | | | |
| at 1952 prices | Billion yuan | | | 60.35 | 60.35[7] | 64.25 | | | | | | | | |
| Fertilizer collected | Million tons | | | | 168.00[29] | | | 1,930.0[29] | | | | | | |

such readjustments the gross agricultural value product remained unchanged.

The 1958 plan adopted by the People's Congress in February of the year was based on the estimated output of 1957. It was, however, replaced in March by a set of much higher targets, not because the 1957 achievements had been underestimated, but because the great-leap movement had become by now national in scope, embracing all lines of production.

---

[a] Potatoes have been converted into grain-equivalents at the ratio of four unit-weights to one.

[b] The "agricultural-value product" covers agriculture, forestry, animal husbandry, agricultural side-occupations and fishery (exclusive of fishing by mechanical means). Handicrafts consumed at the rural source of production and preliminary processing of agricultural products are included in the "over-all agricultural-value product" but not included in the "agricultural-value product."

SOURCES:

[1] Liao Lu-yen, "Final Evaluation of the 1956 Operations in Agricultural Production and Major Tasks for 1957," *HHPYK*, 8: 81–88, April, 1957.

[2] Po I-po, "Report on the Results of the 1956 Plan and on the Plan for 1957," *JMJP*, July 2, 1957.

[3] Po I-po, "Report on the Draft Plan for 1958," *HHPYK*, 5: 12–23, March, 1958.

[4] Bureau of Planning, Ministry of Agriculture, *Chung-kuo yü shih-chieh chu-yao-kuo-chia nung-yeh sheng-chan t'ung chi tzu-liao hui-p'ien* [A Compendium of the Agricultural Statistics of China and other Major Countries of the World], Peiping, October, 1958.

[5] Peiping dispatch, January 5, 1959, *TKP* (Hong Kong), January 6, 1959.

[6] State Statistical Bureau, "Communique on the Results of the 1958 Plan," *JMJP*, April 15, 1959.

[7] State Statistical Bureau, *Wei-ta ti shih-nien*, [The Great Ten Years], Peiping, 1959.

[8] Li Fu-ch'un, "Report on the Draft Plan for 1959," *JMJP*, April 22, 1959.

[9] Chou En-lai, "Report on Revision of the Major Targets in the 1959 Plan and on Stepping up the Movement for Increasing Output and Economizing," *JMJP*, August 29, 1959.

[10] Li Fu-ch'un, "Report on the Draft Plan for 1960," *JMJP*, March 31, 1960.

[11] Hsüeh Mu-ch'iao, "How does Statistical Work make a Great Leap," *TCKT*, 5: 1–5, March, 1958.

[12] Sixth Plenary Session, Central Committee, Chinese Communist Party, "Communique on the National Economic Plan of 1959," *JMJP*, December 18, 1958.

[13] Bureau of Food Crop Production, Ministry of Agriculture, "Food Production during the Period of the First Five-Year Plan," *HHPYK*, 9: 80–83, May, 1958.

[14] NCNA (New China News Agency) release, September 29, 1958.

[15] NCNA release, June 30, 1958.

[16] NCNA release, October 12, 1958.

[17] Wu Po, "Explanations for the Draft Regulations of Agricultural Tax of the People's Republic of China," *JMJP*, June 5, 1958.

[18] Chi Chung-wei, "China's Industry must positively Assist and Promote the Development of Agriculture," *CCYC*, 2: 1–11, February, 1958.

[19] Wang Keng-chin, "Some Points of my Understanding of Agricultural Planning," *CHYTC*, 14: 15–21, November, 1959.

[20] NCNA release, May 17, 1959.

[21] Liao Lu-yen, "Tasks at the 1959 Agricultural Battle Front," *HC*, 1: 11–18, January, 1959.

[22] State Statistical Bureau, "Communique on Correction of the 1958 Agricultural Statistics," *JMJP*, August 27, 1959.

[23] Li Hsien-nien, "Report on the Realized Budget of 1957 and on the Planned Budget for 1958," *HHPYK*, 5: 4, March, 1958.

[24] NCNA release, February 3, 1958.

[25] NCNA release, September 25, 1958.

[26] NCNA release, September 25, 1959.

[27] Chang Mu-yao, "Statement at the National Conference," *JMJP*, April 14, 1960, p. 19.

[28] Chou En-lai, "Report on the Work of the Government," *JMJP*, April 19, 1959.

[29] "People's Communes are Good," *JMJP*, January 4, 1959, p. 5.

The figures in column 6 in the table are merely examples, because the targets were kept rising during the ensuing months. It was during this period that the Ministry of Agriculture issued for the first time communiqués on the national results of the great leap with regard to the output of some crops—results that formed the bases for the later estimates for the whole year.[8] For example, according to one of these communiqués issued in October, the output of rapeseed for the year stood at 1,350,000 metric tons; at the end of the year the estimate was 1,384,500 tons.

As in 1957, the estimates for 1958 published in January, 1959, and the finalized figures released by the State Bureau in April, 1959, were identical or practically identical for such major items as food grains, soy beans, and cotton. But with respect to all other items for which data are available, adjustments from the estimates were substantial, ranging from a reduction of 36 per cent in groundnuts, 32 per cent in sugar cane, 20 per cent in rapeseed, to 13 per cent in jute and hemp, 10 per cent in pigs (in sty), and 3 per cent in sugar beets. Such readjustments from year-end estimates were in line with previous practices, except that here the readjustments were all downward and generally much more substantial.

The revision of the finalized statistics for 1958, announced in August, 1959, is concerned with more specified items. Three of them pertain to the major products whose output estimates had not been adjusted in April but were now scaled down—by one-third for food grains, by 36 per cent for cotton and by 16 per cent for soy beans. Now it was also found that the original claims of output of potatoes had been inflated by 102 per cent, coarse grains by 50 per cent, wheat

---

[8] Ministry of Agriculture, "Communiqué on the 1958 Output of Summer- Harvested Food Grains," *JMJP,* July 23, 1958; "Communiqué on the 1958 Output of Early Rice," "Communiqué on the 1958 Output of Spring Wheat," and "Communiqué on the 1958 Output of Rapeseed," all in *JMJP,* October 13, 1958.

by 38 per cent, and rice by 32 per cent. Three items that
had been reduced in April from the early estimates were now
reduced further: groundnuts, by 30 per cent, pigs by 11 per
cent, and jute and hemp by 1.5 per cent. Two other items,
for which the finalized data given in April are not available,
were now pared down from the original claims to the extent
of 42 per cent (afforested area) and 46 per cent (cured
tobacco). "As a result of the revision of data for the eight
items mentioned above," says the communiqué of the State
Bureau, "the agricultural-value product at 1957 prices was
changed from 88 billion to 67.1 billion yuan, a reduction of
24 per cent." Here it may be inferred that statistics for items
which did not enter into the computation of agricultural-
value product (or, for that matter, of agricultural- and industrial-value product) and which might need equally drastic
revision, were left out of the official statement. Downward
revision was not necessarily confined to those eight items only.
The much-discussed figures on "fertilizer collected" are a
case in point.

What were the reasons officially given for the revision in
August, 1959? Three official statements were made public on
this matter simultaneously on the same day. But in the
order of publication, the statement by the State Bureau came
first (*JMJP*, August 26), followed by that of the 8th Plenary
Session of the Central Committee of the Chinese Communist
party (*JMJP*, August 27) and finally by that of Premier Chou
En-lai at the Standing Committee of the People's Congress
(*JMJP*, August 29). The first two communiqués agreed on
two reasons: (a) "Because of the lack of experience in estimating output under the unprecendented bumper-crop conditions of 1958, the agricultural statistical offices have overestimated in most instances"; and (b) "because of the lack
of proper allocation of the labor force during the huge autumn
harvests, the work of reaping, threshing, gathering, and storing

was so poorly done that some part of the harvest was lost, thus
making the amount harvested different from the estimated
output." To reason (a), Premier Chou referred in terms of
"the lack of experience in estimating output under conditions
of bumper crops in large areas and of sudden, large increases
in unit-area yield." He also added a third reason, namely,
underestimation of the adverse effect of natural calamities on
the output of 400 million $mou^9$ of cultivated land in 1958.

Why should reasons (a) and (c) be of such particular
importance to the statistics of 1958 that the original claims
were inflated more than 100 per cent in several cases? After all,
natural calamities and bumper crops were no new experience,
and the "unprecedented" crop of the year was based precisely
on the exaggerated reports from the field. However, these
apparently lame excuses for the statistical fiasco of 1958 make
sense in the light of what has been brought out in the present
analysis. With statistical reporting placed at the disposal of
local party leaders who were under pressure for a great leap
in output and who were also responsible for conducting
"model surveys" and for making projections on the basis of
such surveys without any operational constraint hitherto
exercised by the state statistical services, all "progress statistics"—always produced at a moment's notice for publicity
and for reporting to higher authorities—were bound to be
running away from reality—all the more so because of the
constant emulation between localities. The situation was ag-
gravated by disruption of the reporting services during the
rise of people's communes in the latter part of the year.
Premier Chou was, therefore, quite informative in his statement of the reasons for revision.

The second reason given—loss in the process of reaping,
threshing, gathering, and storing—is of peculiar interest, because it may be interpreted to mean that the statistics on

---

⁹ Fifteen *mou* equal one hectare.

output for 1958 as revised in August, 1959, refer to barn yield whereas the earlier data pertain to biological yield.[10] However, such a sudden change in the definition of output could not have taken place in 1958. If output data before 1958 refer to barn yield while those of 1958 refer to biological yield, the change could only be interpreted as a nation-wide, concerted act of deliberately deceiving the central authorities— which is not likely. Moreover, why was such an obvious fact not discovered in April, 1959, when the State Bureau had already examined and scaled down the output estimates of many items? And when the fact was allegedly discovered for the August revision, why was the readjustment confined to merely eight items?

If all output data up through 1958 were of biological yield, as they clearly were, why did the August communiqués refer to the loss from harvesting only for 1958 and not for the preceding years? One possible answer might be that the highly inflated progress statistics had caused great difficulties for the state purchasing agencies. On August 30, 1958, Peiping issued a directive calling for the stepping up of government purchases of cotton and tobacco leaves, in which the ouput of cotton (ginned) was estimated to have doubled during the year, and that of tobacco leaves trebled. Acting in line with these estimates, the purchasing agencies might have been running into difficulties with the peasantry. Their frustration would turn into fury directed to none other than the agricultural statistics offices that produced such estimates. Thus, the second reason cited in the official explanation might be primarily addressed to these critics.

However that might be, it is certain that not only were the agricultural-output statistics for 1958 uniquely inflated because of the great-leap movement, but biological yield be-

---

[10] On the basis of estimating agricultural output, see below, pp. 124–125.

gan to differ considerably from barn yield during the year. To measure farm output by biological yield was an established practice in the country, but apparently the discrepancy between biological output and barn yield had never been serious enough to call the practice into question. The reason is not far to seek. Much of the Chinese folklore pounds on the theme that "every kernel of food grain costs a drop of sweat and blood." Such tradition is expected of a densely populated country with family agriculture of the intensive-cultivation variety. Hence, the loss of the harvest from the field to the barn had always been kept at a minimum, making the biological yield virtually identical with barn yield. But communization, by reducing the whole peasantry into a proletariat, began in 1958 to deprive the peasants of the incentive to save every bit of grain in harvest. This is no speculation, for the losses have since grown to an extent that in 1960 local campaigns "to pick up grains from the ground" between the field and the barn were reported in various parts of the country. And the central authorities in Peiping ordered a change in the basis for output statistics from biological yield to barn yield in 1960.[11]

If operationally the statistical services in rural areas were independent of the State Statistical Bureau in 1958, as is argued here, what grounds did the bureau have for scaling down the original estimates of the Ministry of Agriculture? According to the three official statements of August, 1959, checking on the 1958 results was carried out repeatedly in the first half of 1959 by the State Bureau. It is difficult to find out the exact meaning of this checking process. Such technical operations as correction of computation mistakes and elimination of obvious duplications might account for much of the revision in April, 1959. It will be recalled that up

---

[11] Huang Chien-t'o, "Chief Tasks in the Agricultural Statistical Work Program for 1960," *CHYTC*, 2: 18–21, February, 1960.

to that time the early estimates for food grains, raw cotton, and soy beans stood unchanged. Apparently the ministry held fast to the authenticity of these figures. Two developments might have subsequently convinced the ministry of its misplaced confidence. The first was, as we have noted, the frustration of the state purchasing agencies which by the winter of 1958 and the spring of 1959 must have accumulated enough information to show that the ministry's estimates were exaggerations. More important was the second development that followed the national meeting on agricultural statistical work in April, 1959, taking the form of a nation-wide movement of agricultural-output investigations.[12] Unprecedented in scale, the movement was primarily concerned with the quality of agricultural-output statistics for 1958 and for the summer and autumn harvests of 1959.[13]

In any case the checking carried out in the first half of 1959 could not possibly be made against the actual output of 1958. In late July, 1959, the National Conference on the Investigation of the Output of Summer Crops, held at Chengchow, reached the obvious but telling conclusion that "output investigations cannot be separated from the actual process of growth of the crops concerned," otherwise the investigations would be too late to be of value.[14] It is telling because regardless of how the checking on the 1958 output was done in the first half of 1959, the final, revised figures were apparently not as yet regarded as satisfactory by the State Bureau.

The figures for 1959 and 1960 in table 2 also require a few comments. For 1959, when the targets were drastically re-

---

[12] "Report on the National Meeting of Directors of Provincial Statistical Bureaus," *CHYTC*, 8: 1–4, May, 1959. The meeting was held in Peiping, April 11–21.

[13] For details of the movement, see below, chap. x.

[14] "Report on the National Conference on Output Surveys of Summer Harvests," *CHYTC*, 11: 8, August, 1959.

duced in August in order to be in line with the revised figures for 1958, the planned rate of increase was lowered from 40 per cent in food grains, 51 per cent in cotton, 50 per cent in groundnuts, and 39 per cent in agricultural-value product, to only about 10 per cent for each of these items. As for jute and hemp, the originally planned 54 per cent increase was even converted into a planned decrease of 22 per cent. The central authorities had been completely misled by wrong statistical reporting with regard to the potentialities of the "great leap" as well as the achievements. Secondly, the "final" figures for 1959, as announced in March, 1960, were arrived at unusually early; they presumably resulted from the "unprecedented" national agricultural-output investigation movement in the summer and fall of 1959. Thirdly, the Ministry of Agriculture neither issued any more communiqués on crop output as it had done in 1958, nor did it release year-end estimates for 1959 and 1960. Finally, for the first time in all these years no revised plan was made public in 1960, although droughts and typhoons—factors usually responsible for the revision of plans, as in 1957—were already publicized during the summer. In an important sense, all these happenings in 1959 and 1960 were the aftermath of the statistical fiasco of 1958.

INDUSTRIAL STATISTICS

According to Premier Chou's statement of August, 1959, drastic revision of the 1958 statistics that had been finalized four months before was necessary only for the agricultural data since "the industrial-output figures had been verified upon rechecking." Does this mean that the great leap of 1958 and its concomitant developments had no impact on the validity of industrial-output statistics? This is hardly conceivable in view of what happened to agricultural statistics.

Table 3, which was compiled in much the same way as table 2, will furnish the background for discussion.

It will be observed that the final figures for 1957, first made public in April, 1959, were generally (with the exception of machine tools and edible oil) larger than the preliminary estimates. This differs considerably from the situation for the agricultural statistics in 1957 when the estimates and the final figures were identical for items of major importance (food grains, and cotton) and for the over-all agricultural-value product. Moreover, the final results in industrial output were generally larger than planned in the case of producer goods and smaller in the case of consumer goods, thus making it possible for the factory-value product in 1952 prices to be more than the planned product by 8 per cent. This may be compared with the fact that the output of food grains fell short of the target, which had been already lowered in July, by 7 per cent.

In 1958, the great-leap movement began revising the targets for the year continuously upward beginning in March. To keep the central authorities informed of the progress, monthly telegraphic reports were required, in addition to the regular statistical returns, from the business-affairs agencies and important enterprises all over the country. That progress statistics are by nature inflationary should find no exception in the industrial field: The preliminary estimates for 1958, shown in column 6 of table 2, were apparently compiled from the monthly reports, for, unlike those in 1957, many of these year-end estimates were heavily scaled down before the final figures were reached. However, all the readjustments together reduced the over-all industrial-value product only by 2.5 per cent—from 120 million to 117 million yuan. For example, according to the final figures released in April, 1959, the earlier estimates overstated the output of

## Table 3. Selected Industrial Statistics, 1957–1960

| Item | Unit | 1957 | | | 1958 | | | | | 1959 | | | 1960 | |
|---|---|---|---|---|---|---|---|---|---|---|---|---|---|---|
| | | Plan 7/57[1] | Estimated 2/58[2] | Final 9/59[3] | Plan 2/58[3] | Early leap target[4] | Estimated 1/59[5] | Final 4/59[6] | Revised 8/59[3] | Plan 4/59[6] | Plan 8/59[7] | Final 3/60[8] | Plan 3/60[3] | Estimated 1/61 |
| | | (1) | (2) | (3) | (4) | (5) | (6) | (7) | (8) | (9) | (10) | (11) | (12) | (13) |
| Pig iron | Million tons | 5.55 | 5.86 | 5.94 | … | 8.00 | … | 13.69 | 13.69 | 23.00 | … | … | … | … |
| factory | Million tons | … | … | … | … | … | … | … | *9.53* | … | … | 20.50 | 27.50 | … |
| indigenous | Million tons | … | … | … | … | … | … | … | *4.16* | … | … | … | … | … |
| Steel | Million tons | 4.99 | 5.25 | 5.35 | 6.25 | 7.00[a] | 11.00 | 11.08 | 11.08 | 18.00 | 18.00 | 13.35 | 18.40 | 18.45[9] |
| factory | Million tons | … | … | … | … | … | … | … | *8.00* | … | *12.00* | … | … | … |
| indigenous | Million tons | … | … | … | … | … | … | … | *3.08* | … | *6.00* | … | … | … |
| Coal | Million tons | 117.27 | 123.23[11] | 130.73[10] | 150.72 | 168.00 | 270.00 | 270.00 | 270.00 | 380.00 | 335.00 | 347.80 | 425.00 | … |
| factory | Million tons | … | … | *123.23*[12] | … | … | … | … | *218.00*[13] | … | … | … | … | … |
| indigenous | Million tons | … | … | *[7.50]* | … | … | … | … | *51.00*[13] | … | … | … | … | … |
| Electric power | Billion kw-hr | 18.86 | 19.03 | 19.34 | 22.45 | … | 27.50 | 27.50 | 27.53 | 40.00 | 39.00 | 41.50 | 55.50 | 58.00[9] |
| Metal-cutting machine tools | Thousand units | 22.64 | 29.10[14] | 28.00 | 28.20 | 25.05 | 90.00[16] | 50.00[16] | 50.00 | 70.75 | 60.00[17] | 70.00 | 90.00 | … |
| Lumber | Million cu. m. | 25.06 | 25.80[14] | 27.87 | … | … | … | 35.00[16] | 35.00 | … | 38.00[18] | 41.20 | 47.00 | … |
| Cement | Million tons | 6.81 | 6.68[14] | 6.86 | 7.20 | 8.18 | … | 9.30 | 9.30 | 12.50 | … | 12.27 | 16.00 | … |
| Cotton yarn | Million bales | 4.64 | 4.62[19] | 4.65 | 5.20 | … | 6.66[b] | 6.10 | 6.10 | 8.50 | 8.20 | 8.25 | 9.00 | … |
| Cotton cloth[c] | Billion m. | 5.00 | … | 5.05 | … | … | 6.40 | 5.70 | 5.70 | 7.20 | … | 7.50 | 7.60 | … |
| Edible vegetable oil | Million tons | 1.22[20] | 1.45[21] | 1.10 | 1.60 | … | … | 1.25 | 1.25 | 1.80 | … | 1.47 | 1.70 | … |
| Sugar[d] | Million tons | 0.87 | 0.85[22] | 0.86 | 0.94 | … | … | 09.0 | 0.90 | 1.50 | … | 1.13 | 1.30 | … |
| Industrial-value product[e] at 1952 prices | Billion yuan | … | 75.12[19] | 78.39 | … | … | … | … | … | … | … | … | … | … |
| at 1957 prices | Billion yuan | … | 65.64 | … | 74.74 | … | … | … | … | … | … | … | … | … |
| Factory product at 1952 prices | Billion yuan | 60.34 | 62.80[14] | 65.02 | 71.96 | 74.22 | … | … | … | … | … | … | … | … |
| at 1957 prices | Billion yuan | … | 56.18 | … | 64.37 | … | … | … | … | … | … | … | … | … |
| Over-all industrial-value product at 1957 prices[e] | Billion yuan | … | … | 70.40 | … | … | 120.00[23] | 117.00[12] | 117.00 | 165.00[2] | 147.00 | 163.00 | 210.00 | … |

cotton yarn by 9 per cent, cotton cloth by 12 per cent, and machine tools by 80 per cent. Still, whether the final figures had allowed sufficiently for the element of exaggeration in progress statistics is difficult to judge. As expected, most of the items in table 3 gave a final output for 1958 far exceeding the planned quota laid down at the beginning of the great leap. But this cannot be said of such consumer goods as edible vegetable oil and sugar, whose output lagged behind the targets set up even before the great leap for the year. And

---

ᵃ The "great leap" target for steel production for 1958 was later raised to 8–8.5 million tons by the Central Political Bureau of the Chinese Communist Party in May, and further to 10.7 million tons in August, 1958. See *JMJP*, September 1, 1958.

ᵇ In the New Year editorial of the *JMJP* (January 1, 1959), an estimate of 6.8 million bales of cotton yarn was given as the output of 1958.

ᶜ Cotton cloth includes machine-made cloth and those native cloths made of machine-made yarn.

ᵈ Includes the output of handicrafts.

ᵉ Both the "over-all industrial-value product" and the "industrial-value product" refer to the value of output of factory industry and commercialized handicrafts; but the former includes, while the latter excludes, a part of "handicrafts consumed at the rural source of production and preliminary processing of agricultural products."

SOURCES:

[1] Po I-po, "Report on the Results of the 1956 Plan and on the Plan for 1957," *JMJP*, July 2, 1957.

[2] Po I-po, "Report on the Draft Plan for 1958," *HHPYK*, 5: 12–23, March, 1958.

[3] State Statistical Bureau, *Wei-ta ti shih-nien* [The Great Ten Years], Peiping, 1959.

[4] "The Great Leap Forward," *Ts'ai-ching yen-chiu* [Financial and Economic Research], Shanghai, **3: 5,** June, 1958.

[5] Po I-po, "The Tasks at the 1959 Industrial Front," *HC*, 1: 6–10, January 1, 1959.

[6] Li Fu-ch'un, "Report on the Draft Plan for 1959," *JMJP*, April 22, 1959.

[7] Chou En-lai, "Report on Revision of the Major Targets in the 1959 Plan and on Stepping up the Movement for Increasing Output and Economizing," *JMJP*, August 29, 1959.

[8] Li Fu-ch'un, "Report on the Draft Plan for 1960," *JMJP*, March 31, 1960.

[9] Po I-po, "Strive for new Triumphs in the Development of China's Industrial Production," *HC*, 3–4: 19–25, February, 1961.

[10] Cheng Ching-ch'ing, "The Great Achievements of China's Socialist Construction in the Past Ten Years," *CCYC*, 10: 1–10, October, 1959.

[11] State Statistical Bureau, "The Situation of China's Light Industry," *TCYC*, 2: 12–15, February, 1958.

[12] "The Basic Condition of China's Coal Industry," *TCYC*, 4: 18–23, April, 1958.

[13] Chang Lin-chih, "Strive for a High Growth Rate in the Coal Industry," *JMJP*, October 7, 1959, p. 7.

[14] "The Gross Industrial Value Product of China for 1957," *Chin-jih hsin-wen* [Today's News], December 31, 1957.

[15] Sixth Plenary Session, Central Committee, Chinese Communist Party, "Communique on the National Economic Plan of 1959," *JMJP*, December 18, 1958.

[16] State Statistical Bureau, "Communique on the Results of the 1958 Plan," *JMJP*, April 15, 1959.

[17] Editorial, "Strive to meet the Major Targets of the Second Five-Year Plan in the Current Year," *JMJP*, August 27, 1959.

[18] "Struggle for Overfulfilment of the Output Quota for Lumber," *JMJP*, October 20, 1959, p. 3.

[19] Chi Chung-wei, "China's Industry must Positively Assist and Promote the Development of Agriculture," *CCYC*, 2: 1–11, February, 1958.

[20] Li Chu-ch'en, "Report at the People's Congress," *JMJP*, July 12, 1957.

[21] Li Chu-ch'en, "Foster a Great Leap in China's Food Industry," *HHPYK*, 7: 51–53, April, 1958.

[22] Ti Ching-hsiang, "Increase Sugar Output for the People," *TKP*, January 5, 1958.

[23] NCNA release, December 31, 1958, *JMJP*, January 1, 1959.

there were such items as steel and coal, for which the early output estimates were allegedly found accurate enough to require no adjustment.

Although admitting of no error in the 1958 industrial statistics that had been finalized in April, 1959, Peiping, in its official pronouncements in August, 1959, did specify the output of pig iron and steel by indigenous methods in the previous year. This points to the importance of differentiating factory output from "native" production. We have seen that, relatively speaking, the statistical services in large factories and mines had been the best developed during the first five-year plan period, with increasingly more attention being paid to the improvement of primary records at the level of workshops in enterprises.[15] Under the decentralization program and the great-leap movement of 1958, however, great changes were initiated in late April in the management of all state enterprises. These changes have been summarily described by Chairman Liu Shao-chi:

In 1958, through mass movements we carried out the following in our enterprises: readjustment of human relations; establishment of a system in which workers participated in management while cadres participated in labor; close coördination, under the party committee's leadership, of the leading cadres, workers, technical personnel, and managerial staff; and reform, under guidance, of all unreasonable regulations and bylaws.[16]

As a result, the authority of local party committees was greatly enhanced, just as it was in rural areas. Management was soon relegated to such a passive role that Premier Chou had to correct this extreme tendency publicly, describing as "intolerable" the situation where "nobody was responsible for production and development." [17]

[15] See above, pp. 44–46.

[16] Liu Shao-ch'i, "The Triumph of Marxism-Leninism in China," JMJP, October 1, 1959, pp. 2–3.

[17] Chou En-lai, "Report on the Work of the Government," JMJP, April 19, 1959.

Nevertheless, as far as large and medium-sized factories are concerned, the effect of this development on the statistics of their annual output must have been quite different from the effect on agricultural statistics.[18] For, primary records were much more likely to be kept and made available for checking purposes in factories than on farms; and model surveys were not resorted to as frequently and extensively in compiling factory statistics as they were in agricultural statistics. Exaggerations were doubtless made in the progress reports under the pressure of the great-leap movement, but when annual statistical returns were prepared according to the principle of complete enumeration, excessive claims in the monthly or quarterly reports could be detected and corrected. On the whole, the major effect of the great leap on modern-factory output probably manifested itself not so much in inflating output statistics as in widespread product adulteration and quality deterioration which were reflected in statistics as a genuine increase in physical output. This was virtually conceded by the chairman of the State Economic Commission in early 1961:

A leap forward in the quality and variety of industrial output is a major task in the industrial front for the next two or three years. After the output of a product with a given quality has reached a certain level, improvement in quality and increase in assortment become a matter of first importance. . . . The agencies of the heavy-industry and light-industry ministries must set up and strictly enforce quality standards and a system of inspection that will debar inferior products from being sent out of the factory. No enterprise should single-mindedly go after the goals of output-value and output-volume at the sacrifice of quality.[19]

Statistics on production by small factories and by indigenous methods present a totally different picture. Under

<hr />

[18] For definition of size of enterprises and their relative importance, see my *Economic Development of Communist China*, p. 232.

[19] "Strive for New Triumphs in the Development of China's Industrial Production," *HC*, 3–4: 19–25, February, 1961.

the slogan "all people enter industry" that was widely publicized in 1958, production by whatever means was greatly
encouraged; and with the rise of people's communes, followed by the backyard-furnace campaign, the number of
worksheds grew fast. The people working there have since
been known in Peiping terminology as the "small indigenous
group" and the "small nonindigenous group" in contrast to
the large and medium-sized "nonindigenous group" of modern
factories and mines. Statistical services were generally non-
existent in these worksheds; their national output was estimated on the basis of model survey, many of which were
conducted by the *hsien* governments.[20] The importance of
small factories may be gauged from the fact that in 1958 the
total output of the coal industry was 270 million tons, of
which 19 per cent (against less than 6 per cent in 1957) were
produced by indigenous methods, 58 per cent (72 per cent
in 1957) by centrally controlled enterprises, and 43 per cent
by medium and small-sized enterprises.[21] In 1959, 46 per cent
of factory-produced pig iron and 64.6 per cent of factory-
produced steel came from "large-sized" establishments, the
rest from medium- and small-sized ones.[22] As for the small
"native" workshops, a survey was made of the industries operated by the people's communes in seventeen provinces and
special municipalities: In 1958 these industries produced
2,400,000 tons of "indigenous" pig iron, 530,000 tons of "indigenous" steel, 25,300,000 tons of coal, 290,000 tons of
cement, and 36,400,000 kw.-hrs. of electricity.[23] Table 3 shows

---

[20] Wang I-fu, "On the Problem of Improving the System of Industrial
Statistical Returns," *TCYC*, 7: 9–13, July, 1958.

[21] Chang Lin-chih, "Strive for a High Growth Rate in the Coal Industry," *JMJP*, October 7, 1959, p. 7.

[22] See Li Fu-ch'un, "Report on the Draft Plan for 1960," *JMJP*, March
31, 1960.

[23] Ch'ai Mou, "The Superiority of People's Communes from the Viewpoint of Fiscal and Trading Work," *CCYC*, 11: 34–37 and 65, November, 1959.

that for the same year the national total of "indigenous" output reached 4,160,000 tons of pig iron, 3,080,000 tons of steel and 51,000,000 tons of coal. It is not clear whether these national aggregates were estimated from the results of that survey. It seems that while the national figures for pig iron and coal appear plausible on the basis of the results of the survey, the total for steel is certainly way out of line.

In any case the quality of these estimates was well evaluated by the Department of Industrial Statistics of the State Bureau when it commented on the iron and steel output figures of 1958 in these terms:

> Because no statistical recording system has yet been set up or sufficiently strengthened in the "small indigenous group," it is unavoidable that its statistical materials are not accurate enough. But we must verify their figures carefully; and we must be opposed to fabrication.[24]

Thus, even the State Bureau looked upon the figures for production by indigenous methods with skepticism, which should be equally applicable to the reports from small-sized factories. Why is it then that in August, 1959, when the final figures for 1958 were officially revised, the output figures for pig iron and steel were merely broken into "factory" and "indigenous" with no alteration in the global totals (columns 7 and 8 in table 3)? This must have been due to the realization that indigenous production, whose quality is generally far inferior, could not be meaningfully lumped together with factory output, and that since it would be impossible to estimate accurately the indigenous output, the sum of the two was of no significance and therefore not worthy of the trouble of readjustment, which indeed would render all industrial statistics open to question. As a matter of fact, figures for indigenous output have not been separately released since

---

[24] "Strengthen Further the Statistical Work on Iron and Steel," *CHYTC*, 1: 13–15, January, 1959.

1958: either factory output alone is given as in the case of iron and steel, or both factory and "indigenous" output are lumped together as in the case of machine tools and most other products.[25] This latter practice has greatly complicated the problem of evaluating industrial statistics. As to small factories, a serious effort was made, as we will see, by the city statistical bureaus in 1959 and 1960 to set up statistical services for them.[26]

SUMMARY

Decentralization of control over state enterprises and the great-leap movement together gave rise to the national statistical work reform from early summer to October in 1958 that went far to destroy the unified state statistical system and to install local party-committee domination over statistical services. The "reform" was particularly effective in rural areas where the state statistical system had not taken root. In fact, toward the end of 1958, the very existence of the whole state statistical service was threatened. The monthly *T'ung-chi yen-chiu* [Statistical Research], founded in January, 1958, as a more technical publication than *T'ung-chi kung-tso* [Statistical Work] and an addition to it, was discontinued in October of the year. Three months later, even the latter was terminated upon merging with *Chi-hua ching-chi* [Planned Economy], the official journal of the State Planning Commission—on the ground that "planning and statistical work are now being performed by one single office in some provinces and in many special districts and *hsien*." [27]

---

[25] There are exceptions. For example, the figures for total output and for machine-made paper have been made public.

[26] See below, pp. 136–139.

[27] *CHYTC*, No. 1, January, 1959, back cover. As a result of the merger, all discussions on the theory and problems of planned economy were to be published in *Ching-chi yen-chiu* [Economic Research], the journal of the Economic Research Institute of the Chinese Academy of Sciences.

The great leap introduced the method of "planning with two accounts" that entailed a self-acceleration of output targets. As an all-pervasive, intensified emulative campaign, it required the use of progress statistics for planning, publicity, and checking purposes. These figures are inherently upward biased, but were much more so in the agricultural statistics of 1958 because of the enforcement of the "eight-word charter," the wide application of the method of "model survey" and the rise of people's communes. It was the Bureau of Planning in the Ministry of Agriculture that was responsible for compiling preliminary national statistics on agriculture, to be approved and finalized by the State Bureau. For 1958 the original claims for the output of food grains, soy beans, and cotton were first accepted in April, 1959, by the State Bureau as "final," while those for the output of other crops were reduced in varying proportions. Probably mainly because of the increasing difficulties encountered by the tax bureaus and the state purchasing agencies who operated according to the original claims of output, the State Council ordered the State Bureau to organize in April, 1959, an "unprecedented" nation-wide movement of agricultural-output investigation, checking on the quality of statistics for 1958 and for the summer and fall harvests of 1959. The data gathered from this movement, together with the information amassed by the state purchasing agencies, provided the State Bureau with the basis for drastically scaling down in August, 1959, the "final" figures for 1958, especially the output figures of the major crops. However, even the bureau has affirmed that these investigations conducted in 1959 were too late to be of use in readjusting the 1958 statistics; and it has remained far from satisfied with the finally revised agricultural statistics for 1958.

As for industrial statistics, extensive reorganization in the management of state enterprises as well as administrative agencies in 1958 did not seem to produce any serious disruption in their statistical reporting services, the foundation of which had been built up to some extent for a number of years. As expected, the great-leap movement did induce overstatement in progress statistics, but they were adjusted downward in the "final" statistics released by the State Bureau in April, 1959. The major effects of the great leap were found in product adulteration in factory output and inferior product in indigenous output on the one hand and in inflating the figures on production by small factories and by indigenous methods on the other. The State Bureau was helpless in coping with the development, and at least for 1958 it did not consider worthwhile revising the "total" output figures for pig iron and steel. The statistical problem of output by workshops and worksheds is serious because under the policy of "all people enter industry" such production has been increasing in quantitative, if not in relative, importance in total industrial output.

Since the statistics of the small-sized sector bear the brunt of overestimation in progress statistics, it may be said in general of all functional statistics since 1958 that their quality varies inversely with the importance of the "small-sized" component. This rule, as it may be so called, holds true for the statistics before 1958, too, except that without the pressure of the great-leap movement, the figures for the indigenous component might be subject as much to underestimation as to overestimation.

Part Three: The Resurgence

# CHAPTER IX

# The "Partisanship" Principle in Statistics

By the middle of 1959 the central authorities in Peiping must have been convinced that the experience of the fiasco of 1958 had vindicated the unified statistical system Director Hsüeh had been unable to defend against the opposition of local party leaders. One would therefore have expected that the State Bureau would now be given greater support than before in expanding its national network of services and maintaining a direct line of authority over them. Yet, within a month of the announcement of the revision of the 1958 statistics, Hsüeh Mu-ch'iao, founder of the state system, was formally removed from the directorship of the bureau. Why did this happen? What does this development mean to national statistics?

It seems certain that Hsüeh was not made a scapegoat for the fiasco of 1958. As we have seen, the original claims for agricultural output in 1958 were made by the Ministry of Agriculture, and it was the State Bureau that undertook to revise them. When Hsüeh was removed, one of his deputies since 1952, Chia Ch'i-yun, succeeded to the directorship, none of the other deputies left with Hsüeh, and Huang Chien-t'o, chief of the Department of Agricultural Statistics in the Bureau during all these years, stayed on in the same capacity. Had Hsüeh been held responsible for what happened in 1958, the bureau would have been extensively reorganized.

According to all available evidence, Hsüeh was dismissed

probably because of his continuous, if not growing, opposition
to both local party direction of statistical work and the compilation of progress statistics for local focal-point programs at
the sacrifice of national statistics. Hsüeh stated his position in
the last paper he published in the official journal of the bureau
in May, 1959; it was originally a lecture on "Several Important Questions in Statistical Theory" given at the Department
of Statistics of the People's University in Peiping.[1] He started
out with the general proposition that statistics is a science,
and arrived at the conclusion that statistical services must be
rendered by a state statistical hierarchy with unified principles. Thus he did not concede any ground to his critics. In the
course of discussion in the paper, the point was made that
while statistics should be as truly reflective of reality as possible, absolute accuracy is impossible for methodological reasons, and that under certain circumstances, such as during the
period of land redistribution or of agricultural coöperation,
timeliness is more important than accuracy, in which case
only the simplest method such as the model survey, need be
used. On the method of model survey, he admitted the past
mistake of deprecating its usefulness, but cautioned that it
could not take the place of complete enumeration required
by the regular schedules. Thus we are told that all progress
statistics, whether on land reform or agricultural collectivization or communization or great leap in output, should not
be taken at their face value. This attitude, indeed, is based on
an important resolution reached by the national meeting of
provincial bureau directors one month earlier. It said that
completion of the work program set forth by the State Bureau must be assured by all provincial bureaus and other
local offices, which, therefore, should not be overburdened

---

[1] *CHYTC*, 8: 5–9, May, 1959.

with the statistical requirements of local party and government leaders.[2]

It will be recalled that there had long been a group in the statistical working force critical of the competence of the local party and political authorities to interfere with statistical reporting.[3] The experience of 1958 was exactly what this group needed to prove the case. Now with Hsüeh on their side, these critics became vocal. "For a year now," reported Chia, the new director of the State Bureau, in October, 1959, "rightist tendencies have become very serious, as shown by the fact that this spring and summer a part of the working force, complaining about the heavy work load, neglected the work on progress statistics in certain areas, government departments, and enterprises."[4] But the "bitterest" experience, Chia continued, was the fact that statistical reports had been prepared for the sake of statistics without any political guidance, thus providing material for the rightists to attack the regime. As Chou En-lai put it in his statment of August 26, 1959, "In the last two months rightist sentiments have developed, raising doubts concerning mass movements, the great leap, the people's communes, and even the socialist system." It is, therefore, hardly surprising that although Hsüeh's dismissal was announced in September, he had already ceased to function as director of the State Bureau as early as June.[5]

---

[2] "Report on the National Meeting of Directors of Provincial Statistical Bureaus," *CHYTC*, 8: 1–4, May, 1959.

[3] See above, pp. 34 and 42–44.

[4] Chia Ch'i-yun, "Excerpt of the Speech at the National Conference of Directors of Provincial and City Statistical Bureaus," *CHYTC*, 14: 1–5, November, 1959.

[5] This observation is based on the fact that Hsüeh's last article was published in the official journal of the bureau in May, and that in June when an essay on "The Problems of Policy concerning China's Statistical Work" was requested to commemorate the 38th birthday of the Chinese Communist party, it was written by Chia instead of by Hsüeh. It is possible that Hsüeh's position during this period was influenced by

The lack of political guidance was regarded as the crux
of the matter. In June, upon taking up the actual directorship
of the bureau, Chia stated that "the erroneous thinking all
these years" consisted in regarding statistics as a science above
political considerations, taking a purely technical viewpoint
toward statistical work, stressing the professional nature of
the service, and giving exclusive concern and priority to its
own requirements. According to Chia, all this implied rejec-
tion of party leadership, whereas "only the party is qualified
to furnish leadership to statistical work." [6] The April meeting
of provincial bureau directors—when Hsüeh was still director
of the State Bureau—was now criticised for failure to ac-
knowledge this thesis and its implications, all of which are
subsumed under the "principle of partisanship in statistical
services." [7] It was hardly a coincidence that on the heels of
Hsüeh's formal dismissal a national conference of provincial
and city bureau directors immediately convened in Peiping
to adopt this principle as the supreme guide for their work.

In essence, this so-called partisanship principle emphasizes
the idea that statistics should always be taken as a weapon
in the class struggle, and as such should serve the interests
of the working class and the party. Thus stated, the principle
comprehends the nature and functions of statistics as originally visualized by the authorities of the State Bureau.[8] However, it was interpreted at the conference in such a way that

---

Chen Yun, the most important economic planner in the country up to
the summer of 1958 when he fell out with the central authorities—
perhaps in relation to the whole program of communization. Chen was
chairman of the Financial and Economic Commission in the early years
of the regime when Hsüeh served as secretary-general of the commission. Chen got back into the public limelight only in early 1961.

[6] Chia Ch'i-yun, "On the Problems of Policy concerning China's Statistical Work," *CHYTC*, 10: 1–6, July, 1959.

[7] Chia Ch'i-yun, "Final Evaluation of Statistical Work at the National
Conference of Directors of Provincial and City Statistical Bureaus,"
*CHYTC*, 14: 6–8, November, 1959.

[8] See above, pp. 14–15.

much of the previous practice of the bureau was at variance with it. The following deserves to be quoted:

The principle of partisanship has not been well understood in practice and has in fact been violated by those who keep stressing a direct line of authority and the supervising and checking functions of statistics; by those who do not follow the policies and principles of the party in regard to statistical methods [that is, those who favor complete enumeration at the expense of "model survey"]; by those who regard statistics as the work for the trained only, and not for the masses; by those who work on statistics for the sake of statistics, thus detaching themselves from politics and reality, reducing statistical work to the status of a by-stander in relation to the party's work program [that is, refusing to engage in progress statistics]; and by those who take a *laissez-faire* attitude toward anti-party attacks and toward statistical data that misrepresent facts.[9]

Strict adherence to the partisanship principle, therefore, requires a radical change in the statistical system. This must be what was meant when it was reported that at the October conference close integration of the system into party leadership was achieved "through incorporating the partisanship principle in the organization and leadership of the statistical service, in the formulation of statistical methods, and in the collection, compilation, and application of statistical materials." [10]

Needless to say, the action to reaffirm the partisanship principle was not taken for the purpose of furthering the control of the central party authorities. In a Communist state, this would be unnecessary. As a matter of fact, the central authorities were called on to give explicit support to the State Bureau in its early effort to build up the state system.[11] With-

---

[9] Chuang Chung, "Evaluation of the Experience from Strengthening Partisanship in Statistical Services, and Raising the Theoretical Level of China's Statistics," *CHYTC*, 2: 35 and 21, February, 1960.

[10] *Ibid.*

[11] See above, p. 35 ff.

out central approval, the system could not have existed, let
alone develop the way it did. If meaningful, the action in
question must have been taken on behalf of local party leadership, which, having gained control over statistical work in
1958, was running into strong opposition in 1959. This speculation has been substantiated by an editorial in the February,
1960, issue of the joint official publication of the State Planning Commission and the State Bureau, which says: "In accordance with the partisanship principle, all statistical personnel must place their work under the absolute direction of the
party: whatever data the local party committee needs and
however and whenever it wants them should be promptly
complied with." [12]

Did this reaffirmation of local party-committee domination
lead to further deterioration of national statistics in 1959
and after? The answer could not be given in definite terms.
The new director of the State Bureau, while introducing the
partisanship principle to statistical work, stressed at the same
time the necessity of a national, specialized agency to be
responsible for conducting the services. Three reasons were
advanced, namely, the unified nature of the work (definition
of indicators, computing methods, pricing, and so on), the
unified leadership in the organizing of comprehensive surveys,
and the regular compilation of comprehensive statistics. Chia
rightly criticized the prevailing practice of differentiating the
state statistical service from the services in the business-
affairs system; all of them were now integrated under the
leadership of the state statistical office at every level of local
government.[13] The state system was thus broadened to em-
brace all statistical services in the country—an achievement
that the early founders of the bureau dared not hope for.

To the central authorities in Peiping the debacle of 1958

---

[12] Editorial, "Statistical Services also Require Technological Innovation by the Masses," *CHYTC*, 2: 30–31, February, 1960.
[13] Chia, "On the Problems of Policy," as cited in note 6.

must have driven home the lesson that planning requires satisfactory national statistics which at the present stage can best be administered by a national service with a set of unified principles. Because of the practical problems of tax collection and state purchasing, the lesson must have also been increasingly appreciated by the local party and political authorities. In April, 1959, at the direction from Peiping, the national meeting of provincial statistical bureau directors resolved to make quality improvement of statistical services the major task for 1959. As a result, most of the party committees and people's commissions at provincial and city levels in the country undertook to check on the quality of statistical materials for 1958 and the first half of 1959, and, through this, to reform the services in rural areas and in industrial and mining enterprises, to reinforce the centralized control of statistical schedules and statistical figures, and to establish a set of far more reasonable statistical regulations.[14]

If the fiasco of 1958 had proved the worth of the state statistical system, the development in the party's internal politics must have aided the restoration and expansion of the operational authority of the system. It will be recalled that ever since the decentralization program was put into effect in early 1958 there had been a growing conflict between national interests and local initiative, as manifested by the desire of local party committees to run their own affairs with the minimum restraint from the center. As a counter measure, Peiping at first stressed the theme that the development of the national economy is like a game of chess in which every move has to be considered in relation to other moves and no one should get out of step with the others.[15] Then, the antirightist

---

[14] Chia, "Excerpt of the Speech . . ." as cited in note 4.

[15] See, for example, Ou Ming, "On the Whole Country as a Game of Chess," *CHYTC*, 2: 3–4, January, 1959; editorial, " 'The Whole Country as a Game of Chess' is the Basic Assurance to Realize the 1959 Leap-Forward Plan," *CHYTC*, 4: 1–2, February, 1959.

campaign was announced in August, 1959 against all those not in sympathy with the major policies of the center. Local party committees, however, continued to be so recalcitrant that in January, 1961, Peiping decided to establish six "central bureaus" in various parts of the country, "representing the central authorities to exercise stronger central party leadership over the party committees at the provincial level." [16]

What all this meant to statistical services is that with central support the State Bureau began to extend its operational responsibility all the way to the countryside in 1959, its offices in full charge of statistical work at the various levels of local government. In a sense, the affirmation of the partisanship principle toward the end of 1959 was itself part of Peiping's effort to find a *modus vivendi* whereby the bureau would be able to maintain a direct line of command over the statistical staff at various local levels without antagonising local party leadership. Significantly, it was in late December, 1960, on the eve of the establishment of the "central bureaus," that Hsüeh was reinstated as a senior deputy chairman of the all-important State Planning Commission, a post he had held concurrently with his directorship of the State Bureau from 1952 through 1958.[17]

In another sense the partisanship principle was introduced explicitly to serve the party's interest, particularly to make sure that statistical materials would not be used against the regime as allegedly they were in the summer of 1959. This meant strengthening the authority of local party leaders to

---

[16] The six regions are the Northeast, the North, the East, the Center-south, the Southwest, and the Northwest. See "Communiqué of the Ninth Plenary Session of the Central Committee of the Chinese Communist Party," *JMJP*, January 21, 1961.

[17] In October, 1958, Hsüeh was appointed to be one of the deputy chairmen of the State Economic Commission, although he remained in the directorship of the bureau until June, 1959. It is interesting to note that Chia, as director of the bureau, has neither been appointed to the State Planning Commission nor to the less important State Economic Commission. See also note 5, above.

review all statistical figures. How this authority has been used and what the effect has been on the validity of statistics are difficult to judge. The following remark, made by the party secretary and governor of Shansi province at the provincial statistical conference in 1959, illustrates the view of local party and government leadership:

At the present, in some places and some fields statistical figures are so lacking in accuracy, with estimates made without the necessary basic data, that some figures are changeable at will. In some cases the statistical worker, afraid that he might be criticised for rightist conservatism, even prepared two different sets of figures representing two different levels of growth and let the user choose between them.

From now on, all important comprehensive statistical figures, whether for publication, for internal use, or for reporting to higher authorities, must be consistent with those prepared by the local statistical office. These latter figures, in turn, must be subject to mass supervision [that is, mass participation in reporting, and making the figures known to the masses concerned], and should be finalized by the local party and government leaders. When there is disagreement between the local statistical office and the local leaders, could the former present its case to the latter? The answer is positive. Provided the opinion is based on facts, the leaders might accept it.[18]

It will be noted that aside from confirming the new role of the state statistical system, the speaker strongly implied that finalization of statistical figures by local leaders would both discourage irregular practices on the part of the working force and improve the quality of statistics. On the other hand, since the question was raised as to what the local statistical office might do in case of disagreement it was clear that most participants in the conference had had frustrating experiences of this kind, especially in 1958; and that the question was hotly discussed during the conference and was regarded as serious

---

[18] Wei Heng, "Develop the Practice of Verification and Establish Accurate Statistical Services," *CHYTC*, 6: 1–3, March, 1959.

enough to call for an answer from one who represented local Party and government leadership.

The view of the local offices of the state statistical system is given by the new director of the State Bureau in his final summing up at the national conference in early November, 1959. Not only statistical work programs and statistical methods should follow the dictates of party leaders, said he, but

Statistical materials should also be applied in accordance with the party's demands. Make the figures accurate, verify them, and indulge in no falsification and fabrication. . . . To make the figures accurate requires a process of examining, studying, and checking with related departments and authorities at all levels: we must neither blindly trust that all figures submitted by the statistical office below are absolutely correct, nor steadfastly uphold these figures without open-mindedly taking into account the opinions from all sides, party leaders in particular. Otherwise, we would be all wrong. To take statistical figures as the only point of departure is in itself an objectivist tendency devoid of political viewpoint or class platform.[19]

A comparison of these two authoritative statements shows that whereas the governor of Shansi would have all statistical figures finalized by the local party and government leaders, the State Bureau merely directed that each local statistical office should take the opinion of local party leaders into account. Most probably, this anomaly means that the figures published at, say, provincial levels are necessarily those locally finalized but may not be those that enter into calculations of national statistics, which are based on materials available within the state statistical hierarchy. Thus, national statistics, though themselves subject to the approval of the State Council, may not reflect the effects of local party manipulation. In any case, if local party-committee approval tightens up

---

[19] Chia Ch'i-yun, "Final Evaluation of Statistical Work at the National Conference of Directors of Provincial and City Statistical Bureaus," *CHYTC,* 14: 6–8, November, 1959.

working discipline among the statistical staff, and if local statistical offices do put up resistance against alleged manipulations of data by local party and government leaders, the result should be an improvement in the quality of statistics, provincial as well as national.

Another effect of the application of the partisanship principle on statistics has been the change in policy with respect to the publication of statistical materials. Formerly, statistical materials, except "state secrets," were released to the public as soon as they were in order and reasonably accurate.[20] But now the decisions to publish and what to publish have to be examined on the basis of the party's interests. In the words of the State Bureau director, "statistical work should take as its major task the reporting of achievements and triumphs"; as regards failures and reverses, "the question is, reporting to whom under what circumstances."[21] Troubles, therefore, should not be publicized in statistics by the statistical offices. This may be the main explanation why so little statistical information has been released since the great leap of 1958. If this is so, may it be said that the volume of the flow of statistics from Peiping—quite apart from the problem of their quality—is a barometer of the successes and failures of the regime, including the internal unity of the party and its self-confidence as the governing body of the country?[22]

[20] See above, p. 56.

[21] Chia, above, note 19.

[22] Late in July, 1961, the New China News Agency reported that the State Statistical Bureau had been again reorganized during the month. Chia Ch'i-yun, the exponent of the "partisanship" principle in statistics, was dismissed from the bureau's directorship, to be replaced by Wang Szu-hua, a professional statistician and one of the deputy directors of the bureau since its inception. At the same time, Ch'ang Ch'eng, chief of the Department of Comprehensive Statistics, and Wang I-fu, chief of the Department of Industrial Statistics, were promoted to the deputy directorship of the bureau. It seems that the technical character of statistical work is once again fully recognized. However, this reorganization is far too early to be evaluated. For the news release, see *JMJP*, July 24, 1961.

# CHAPTER X

# The National Movement of Agricultural-Output Surveys

Early in 1959, when the central authorities realized that the farm output of 1958 had been badly exaggerated, they instructed the State Bureau and its local offices to mobilize, under local party leadership, all possible resources to check on the data for 1958 and the first half of 1959. For this purpose a national meeting on agricultural statistics convened in Peiping in April, 1959, at the same time as the national conference of provincial bureau directors. The meeting set off a national movement "of unprecedented scale" whose importance should not be underestimated.

The movement called for a concerted effort to investigate the output of major farm products, especially food grains, cotton, and oil-bearing crops. Surveys were conducted by specialized committees, organized at every level from province and special district through *hsien* to commune and production brigade. Chaired by the local party secretary, the committee comprised all officers in charge of the various business-affairs departments; but it was the state statistical officer at that level who was responsible for the functioning of the committee. Local party leadership was considered vital, because without it not only could the committee not be organized properly, but mobilization of the cadres, experienced peasants, activists, and accountants would be impossible. The local party secretary, of course, would not be interested in the role of active leadership unless the surveys to be undertaken by the committee would serve his immediate needs in connection with the local focal-point program, which generally concerns preliminary and final distribution of "income" among commune members, allocation of tax and state-purchase quota, and checking on the production and marketing plans. Since all this requires estimation and verification of farm output, there was no conflict of interest between the local party secretary and the survey committee, and it was not difficult for the local statistical office to enlist his active leadership.

These survey committees were proposed before by the State Bureau at the end of the first five-year plan; but because local party leadership was not sought after, they were not organized in most localities. Now, with local party secretaries at the head of the survey committees, the movement became national in scope and unprecedented in scale. In Anhwei province, for instance, more than 300,000 investigators (including 5,100 full-time) were engaged in surveying the summer harvests, and more than 440,000 (6,100 full-time) in surveying early and mid-autumn harvests.[1]

The method of investigation was outlined at the national meeting of provincial bureau directors in April. Surveys were confined to major crops and their important production areas. The investigators lived and worked together with the peasants at the communes and production brigades, making it possible to integrate the survey work with production. The entire investigation was generally broken into four stages, starting with estimating cropped area and output, usually by means of visual observation, during the period of crop growth. These estimates—aside from serving the needs of those engaged in tax collection, state purchasing, and preliminary distribution within the communes—furnished the basis for the second

---

[1] Planning Commission, Anhwei Province, "Preliminary Evaluation of Surveys of Agricultural Output of 1959 in Anhwei Province," *CHYTC*, 2: 22–26, February, 1960.

stage, namely, dividing the production areas into types in accordance with their estimated productivity and then choosing from each type a small "model area" judged to be representative of it. With harvest came the third stage that centered on sample cutting on each one of the "model areas." As the final stage, total output was computed by applying the results of the cutting surveys to the model areas and then to whole areas.

The output thus arrived at was based on biological yield. This, indeed, had been the general practice in the country since the 1930's. Now, obviously because of the experience of 1958, the national meeting also suggested that "after reaping and threshing, the actual output should also be comprehensively tabulated." [2] This was biological yield, *minus* losses in reaping and threshing. In some provinces, such as Anhwei, the biological yield was later checked against the amount that had actually gone into the barn instead. While estimates of output on the basis of barn yield were thus sporadically resorted to, it was at the Chengchow conference in July, 1959 that the State Bureau began to introduce the policy of "gradual extension of the use of barn-yield statistics." [3] As we have seen earlier, only in 1960 did the central party authorities rule that barn yield was to be the measure of output instead of biological yield.[4]

The survey method as outlined above is, of course, full of pitfalls. With these in mind, the meeting went on to emphasize that the total cropped area be carefully verified; that surveys be separately made of the outcrop in experimentation plots,

---

[2] "Report on the National Meeting of Directors of Provincial Statistical Bureaus," *CHYTC*, 8: 1–4, May, 1959.

[3] The use of barn yield as the basis for computing output was reported in Anhwei province for 1958. See Chang Chen (deputy director of the provincial statistical bureau of Anhwei), "Several Problems of Sampling in Agricultural-Output Surveys," *TCYC*, 4: 27–31, April, 1958.

[4] Huang Chien-t'o, "Chief Tasks in the Agricultural Statistical Work Program for 1960," *CHYTC*, 2: 18–21, February, 1960.

in large high-yield areas, and in average fields; and, above all, that reliance be placed on the local party committee's educational work "to avert the tendency of exaggeration and concealment" by the cadres and the masses.

The detailed accounts of the surveys conducted in Anhwei and Shansi provinces show that these procedures were generally followed.[5] Probably the same situation would be found in other provinces. When the State Bureau convened a national conference on output surveys of summer harvests at Chengchow in late July, it was said that the statistical figures on the summer harvests were "more accurate, more detailed, and more timely" than ever before, although some of the model surveys produced results that were not representative of the groups concerned. The conference called for greater attention to be paid to sample cutting than to visual observation. The general lesson drawn by the conference from the several months of experience was that survey work could neither be separated from the process of crop growth nor from the focal-point programs of the locality.[6]

The importance of the experience of these surveys in 1959 cannot be denied. According to the State Bureau, this national movement of agricultural-output survey opened up a "new, lively era" for rural statistical work that had long been the stumbling block to the development of an effective national statistical network. It was claimed that not only did the timing and quality of reporting improve, but the entire statistical services in the rural areas, from organization to the work program, were led to take a great leap forward.[7] Moreover, in evaluating the importance of the movement for the future,

<hr/>

[5] Planning Commission, *op. cit.*; Wu Kwong-t'ang (deputy governor of Shansi province), "Experience in Agricultural-Output Surveys," *CHYTC*, 11: 6–7, August, 1959.

[6] "Report on the National Conference on Output Surveys of Summer Harvests," *CHYTC*, 11: 8, August, 1959.

[7] Editorial, "The Necessity of Bringing about an All-Front Leap in Rural Statistical Work," *CHYTC*, 2: 4–6, February, 1960.

the chief agricultural statistical officer of the bureau reached
the following conclusion:

From the surveys conducted in the summer and fall of 1959 and
the experience in all these years, we have gained one basic experience with regard to farm-output investigations in China. On
the one hand, investigations should be made under political gen-
eralship and party leadership, with mass participation, but in the
charge of the statistical department. On the other hand, investigations, merging with production at the start, should be closely integrated with the focal-point program of the locality, and proceed
to verify statistical figures, by stages, by groupings, and by crops
in accordance with local agricultural conditions—through coör-
dinating the results gathered from [model survey] points with those
from large areas, improving the quality of preliminary estimates,
doing a good job in crop cutting, and developing barn-yield statistics.

This basic conclusion is crystallized from ten years of experience,
especially 1959, involving millions of workers. It is now the guiding principle and basic direction of all farm-output surveys for
China. In the future, our determination to conduct these surveys
in full accord with this principle must not be weakened in the
slightest degree.[8]

Thus, farm-output surveys have become part of the foundation for agricultural statistics since 1959.

---

[8] Huang Chien-t'o, *op. cit.*

# CHAPTER XI

# The Rural Statistical Network

We have seen that within one and a half months after the Central Committee of the party made the decision in August, 1958, about 98 per cent of all rural households were organized into people's communes.[1] Such quick development was more nominal than actual. When consolidation began at the turn of the year, Peiping issued a directive on the establishment of "accurate statistical services" in the people's communes. This represents China's most serious attempt in extending the statistical network to the countryside.

In general, a commune is divided into several "production control areas," more often known as "production brigades," each being an economic unit accounting for the profits and losses of all its component parts, namely, "production teams" (and their equivalent) that are engaged in materially productive (or service) activities. There are thus three levels of administration within a commune: the highest is the "control commission" that operates a number of functional departments (agriculture, water conservation, forestry, livestock, industry and communications, public finance and food, trade, culture and education, labor, militia, planning); the next two levels, in a decreasing scale of organization, are the management committees of production brigades and of production teams. In a sense, these three levels correspond to the previous district (*ch'u*), town and *hsiang*, and village or large

---

[1] See above, pp. 87–88.

collective. In 1959, there were "more than 20,000 communes, several hundreds of thousands of basic economic-accounting units (brigades), and several millions of production-contract units (teams)." [2]

Directed by the provincial statistical bureaus, the organizational drive was to install statistical officers at the three levels in the communes.[3] According to various reports, the organization structure for statistical work in the communes, while varying in detail from place to place, presents a common outline, in which the application of the partisanship principle is unmistakable.[4] Among the many departments and committees of the commune control commission is the committee of planning and statistics, headed by the local party secretary who, concurrently as deputy chairman of the commune, is in a position to coördinate the work of the committee with the needs of all the departments in the commission. The chief statistical officer of the committee, a specialized, full-time worker, is responsible for compiling progress statistics and preparing regular statistical returns for the state statistical system; he may be assisted by one to three full-time staff members. At the level of production brigade, the commander serves as chairman of a smaller planning and statistical committee, composed of those in charge of operational responsibilities at that level, together with some of the statistical reporting workers at the team level. Like the committee at the control commission, it also engages a full-time statistical worker who used to be either secretary or statistical officer of a *hsiang*. At the team level, there is a permanent part-time statistical reporter, paid or unpaid, in each production team,

[2] Huang Chien-t'o, "Chief Tasks in the Agricultural Statistical Work Program for 1960," *CHYTC*, 2: 18–21, February, 1960. See also Table 1.
[3] "Statistical Services in the Rural Communes are being Initiated," *CHYTC*, 2: 20, January, 1959.
[4] See accounts given in *CHCC*, October, 1958; *TCKT*, September, 1958; *CHYTC*, February, 1960; and *CHYTC*, May, 1960.

educational and cultural unit, commune factory, and financial and trading establishment. This whole statistical organization within the commune is operationally also subject to the direction of the statistical office of the *hsien* government.[5] The objective of the organizational drive was not only to set up services within each commune, but to attain full integration of statistical work within the rural network that comprises the services of all four specified levels.

According to the State Bureau three operational systems were to be introduced to the statistical services in the communes, namely, original records, permanent files of statistical materials, and statistical schedules and figures. The original record system is regarded as the most basic of the three. Not to be confused with the primary record system that deals with such records as vouchers and receipts in industrial and trade statistics, the original record system refers to records of such items as changes in population, cultivated land, agricultural implements, domestic animals and poultry, cropping, and farm management. These records have not been kept before. It has been pointed out that the introduction of the system requires three steps: first, to criticize in a mass meeting the general feeling that such recording takes too much time and serves no purpose; second, to draw up recording regulations in accordance with the needs of production, management, and focal-point programs, and to designate those responsible for the tasks; and third, to continue to improve these regulations as management improves.[6] Recording is to be done by the Worker on the job or the group leader as designated. Without mass participation, therefore, the system of original records is not feasible. The system of permanent files provides the only way to check on the accuracy of sta-

---

[5] See above, pp. 79–80.

[6] Szechwan Provincial Statistical Bureau, "Basic Evaluation of the Work in Establishing Accurate Statistical Services in People's Communes in Szechwan Province," *CHYTC*, 2: 26–29, February, 1960.

tistical figures; it is also something new to the rural scene. The system of statistical schedules and figures is one that the State Bureau has long attempted to enforce on a national scale. In close coödination with those in charge of the business-affairs departments, the chief statistical officer of the commune is given the power to exercise complete control over the dissemination of statistical schedules and figures.

The expansion of such a network to cover more than 80 per cent of the population has been slow, even though some of the past difficulties have been eased. It will be recalled that up to 1957 a major obstacle facing the bureau in its effort to extend its work to the *hsien* level and below was the fact that the local authorities did not understand the importance of statistical work and that the statistical workers, far from being fully occupied in statistical reporting throughout the year, were frequently reassigned to other work and therefore had never acquired any professionalized status in the minds of the peasantry.[7] Now the debacle of 1958 and the continuous need for statistics in relation to focal-point programs had gone far to educate the local leaders about the value of statistical services. The prejudice of the peasantry was partly overcome when statistical workers, like other governmental employees, were required to work in the production front. In 1959 many people's communes in Szechwan province "voluntarily" entered into covenants that generally provided for accepting party leadership and supporting specialization in statistical work.[8]

The development in a few provinces has been reported with some detail. In Szechwan, the most populated province in the country, there were 68,000 full- and part-time statistical workers in all the 5,427 rural communes and 54,947 brigades in the province in early 1960; in addition, hundreds of thou-

---

[7] See above, pp. 73–75.
[8] Szechwan Provincial Statistical Bureau, *op. cit.*

sands of persons had been designated to be responsible for statistical reporting, along with their regular production duties, in more than 270,000 production teams and in such other fields as veterinary medicine, general medicine, and education. This entire rural statistical working force was chosen from among the cadres who had a relatively high degree of political understanding, a strong sense of responsibility, good relations with the masses, and an elementary ability for computation. After one year of effort, the provincial statistical bureau was able to report that 20 per cent of the communes in the province had a statistical organization advanced enough to be equipped with a workable system of original records, 50 per cent had a functioning organization with an original record system for the major production units, 20 per cent had just started their statistical service and the recording systems, and the last 10 per cent had begun the service without a recording system as yet.[9]

In Shansi province a special effort was made in the spring of 1960 to build up the service in the rural areas. During those few months, despite a purge of nearly 5,000 workers for reasons of incompetency and antisocialist sentiments, the total number of professionalized statistical workers in the countryside increased from 100,000 to 110,000, with an increase of full-time workers among them from 12,000 to 27,000. All the control commissions of the communes in the province averaged two statistical workers each, and the production brigades one to two each. In the production teams those who had formerly kept records of work units for the members were now generally converted into the statistical staff. Depending on the importance of their work, nearly 79,000 of these professionals had been given training by the provincial statistical bureau (1,000), by the statistical offices at the special-district and *hsien* levels (10,000), and by the communes themselves

---

[9] *Ibid.*

(68,000). The activist elements in the working force also grew in importance: the percentage of party and youth corps members increased from 47 to 54, and that of poor peasants and lower middle peasants from about 60 to 75. Besides these so-called professionals, there were tens of thousands of voluntary, unpaid statistical workers who had been mobilized to serve in various enterprises and agencies; 59,000 of them had received some training. In the whole province 2,552 statistical schools were newly set up, in addition to the 1,130 that had already been in operation. As a result of all this effort, at the end of spring 95 per cent of all rural communes were able to attain consistency between original records and statistics; 91 per cent had established a permanent file system for statistical materials, and 97 per cent were practicing unified control over schedules and figures.[10]

Such progress as had been made in Szechwan and Shansi provinces, however, was found in only three other provinces (Shensi, Honan and Liaoning) in early 1960.[11] Even in a rich well-developed province like Chekiang, neither original records nor statistical network had been introduced in the countryside, and all basic schedules were yet to reach the primary levels in the communes.[12] And it should be added that in early 1960 "there are still some *hsien* [not to mention communes] where statistical organization and personnel do not meet the demands of the situation." [13]

Thus for 1960 the State Bureau urged all rural communes to install, even in skeleton form, the original record system, the system of permanent files for statistical materials, and the system of schedules. And the bureau itself would make an

[10] Li Fei-tang, "A New Phase of Rural Statistical Work," *CHYTC*, 5: 9–10 and 36, May, 1960.

[11] Editorial, "The Necessity of Bringing about an All-Front Leap in Rural Statistical Work," *CHYTC*, 2: 4–6, February, 1960.

[12] "Training Course for the Statistical Workers of People's Communes in Chekiang Province," *CHYTC*, 2: 9, February, 1960.

[13] Huang, *op. cit.*

attempt during the year to arrange for the whole rural statistical working force to receive training at least once—through
such devices as briefing on one particular operation at a time;
holding long conferences with short periods of training; conducting field inspection; schooling after working hours; and
setting up short-term training courses.[14] Needless to say, the
training program aimed to impart not more than the basic
knowledge to handle the regular schedules.[15]

The statistical work program has also been slowly but
steadily developed in rural areas. Before 1958 all work on
rural statistics was concerned with agriculture only. With the
rise of communes comes the policy of comprehensive development of the rural economy and therefore the need for a statistical service that would compile figures for all functional fields,
especially industrial output and transportation. Since all these
economic activities are so decentralized and scattered in the
countryside, both a huge statistical reporting force and co-
operation from the masses are necessary. Thus, like the
national movement of farm-output surveys, the establishment
of rural statistical services cannot be successful unless local
party committee secretaries are interested enough to assume
active leadership. In 1959 and 1960 the State Bureau repeatedly instructed its workers in the field "to seek active leadership from local party committees." To devise the original
record system according to the needs of production, management, and focal-point programming is obviously intended to
enlist the full support of the local party committee. Moreover, as a principle, the work program of the rural service
has been designed to revolve around progress statistics in
relation to the focal-point programs initiated by local party
leaders.

---

[14] *Ibid.*
[15] "Report on the National Meeting of Directors of Provincial Statistical Bureaus," *CHYTC*, 8: 1–4, May, 1959.

While active local party leadership is thus drawn to promoting the development of rural statistical services, it has also given rise to an alarming consequence. Because of the vast difference in timing, coverage, and computing methods, the statistical personnel have tended to regard progress statistics as quite distinct from the regular statistical returns, and have, indeed, spoken of "two separate accounts." Sometimes, the work on progress statistics has led to statistical surveys that produced a third account of figures. The danger of this situation has apparently been widely recognized. For example, as a target for 1960, the Shansi provincial statistical bureau requested its rural statistical offices to make a serious effort to achieve consistency among progress statistics, regular statistical returns, and statistical surveys. Nationally, the installation in the communes of unified control over statistical figures is meant to serve the same purpose.

The development of rural statistical services has also resulted in reinforcing the operational leadership of the State Bureau, which in 1960 began to exercise the direct control it had sought for many years. According to a Peiping directive early in the year, the bureau was authorized to examine the existing statistical schedules in use in the rural areas with a view to large-scale simplification, and no government department was permitted from then on to send any schedules to the communes without first presenting them to the state statistical office at the same administrative level for checking against duplication and for approval. This goes a long way to reduce the work load of the statistical workers in the communes and to standardize the definition of indicators in the schedules.[16] Furthermore, realizing that the method of "model survey" is going to stay because of its simplicity, but in order to avoid

[16] For the flood of statistical schedules resulting from the great leap of 1958, see editorial, "Strengthen the Control over Statistical Schedules and Overcome the Present Situation of Too Many Schedules," *CHYTC*, 9: 1–2, June, 1959.

the pitfalls that trapped the Ministry of Agriculture in 1958, the State Bureau was prepared in 1960 to choose, as fixed "model reporting units," a number of *hsien,* communes, production teams, and common mess halls that are considered to be representative in each of the provinces. The bureau would establish direct working relations with them, assisting them in improving their statistical personnel and making use of them both as basic reporting units in all "model surveys" and as experimental stations for statistical methods. As for regular statistical reporting, the bureau recommended that the same scheme of designating fixed model reporting units be adopted by all local party committees in rural areas.[17] In addition, the bureau requested that "model surveys be coördinated with complete enumeration," by which is meant that the statistical office at any level, upon receiving the comprehensive returns from below, is required to verify them by organizing surveys in the major producing units and then to submit them to the next level with an evaluation, or, if necessary, with the approval of the local party committee.

It was announced early in 1960 that during the year the bureau would undertake a national check on the development of the rural statistical services and their quality. Its operational leadership has thus finally reached the primary levels in the countryside.

---

[17] This practice had already begun in some provinces in early 1959, apparently with no significant results. Hence, the recommendation to the local Party committee. See "Statistical Services in the Rural Communes . . . ," *op. cit.*

# CHAPTER XII

# Statistical Services in the Cities and Urban Communes

In the earlier discussion of industrial statistics for 1958, it was pointed out that statistical services for the "small indigenous and nonindigenous group" did not then exist. The development of the rural statistical network since then should begin to fill the gap. To complete the picture, a word should be said about the development in the cities where a large number of small workshops have been operating side by side with the large and medium-sized enterprises.

In 1959 and 1960 two major developments took place worthy of special attention. One was "mass participation in statistical work" in various enterprises as a result of the great-leap movement of 1958. Industrial workers, instead of professional statistical personnel, were organized to participate in statistical work along with their regular jobs—by way of keeping primary records, preparing reports on the productive processes, operating as an economic intelligence network, and competing with one another on the basis of statistical showing.[1] All this may be regarded as a device to impress on the industrial workers the importance of statistical work and to secure their indispensable coöperation in the keeping of primary records. If successful, it would accomplish one of the urgent tasks that the State Bureau had set before itself at the beginning of the second five-year plan.

---

[1] Teng Chung-yi (director of the statistical bureau of the city of Taiyuan), "Basic Experience from Organizing City Statistical Services for an All-Front Great Leap," *CHYTC*, 5: 15–19, May, 1960.

The other development was the extension of statistical services to urban communes that first came into existence in the fall of 1958 and had since grown to "more than 1,000" up to August, 1960.[2] These communes were organized primarily for promoting small-scale industrial production as well as for enlarging industrial labor supply, although according to official announcement another primary objective was to remove the last traces of private ownership of means of production. A survey of forty-three cities has shown that at the end of 1959 some 56,000 industrial units had been established in the communes, engaging nearly two million persons, with an annual output worth more than two billion yuan.[3] The way in which statistical services were established in these communes is illustrated by the experience in the city of Chengchow, Honan province.[4]

At the start of the rural commune movement in August, 1958, Chengchow also began to organize itself into 126 small urban communes, claiming as members more than 97 per cent of all those who should belong. By early 1960, these small units had merged into 17 primary-level communes, under which were 126 subsidiary communes and 27 agricultural production brigades. There were also 580 common mess halls, 273 nurseries and kindergartens, 14 old-folks homes, and more than 1,000 servicing stations. The total membership of all the 17 primary-level communes was not announced, but it was reported that 3 of them had more than 60,000 people each,

---

[2] Editorial, "Celebrate our Great National Anniversary," *JMJP*, October 1, 1960.

[3] In addition, according to the survey, the communes made available to the large state industrial enterprises and agencies a labor force of 3,400,000, of whom 80 per cent were women. See Li Hsieh-po, "The Working Class and Urban Communes," *JMJP*, April 9, 1960, p. 2; and Li P'ing-heng, "Unlimited Advantages of Organized Living," *JMJP*, April 9, 1960, p. 18.

[4] Kuo Yung-hua (director of the city statistical bureau of Chengchow), "The Establishment and Development of Statistical Services in the Urban Communes of Chengchow," *CHYTC*, 5: 20–21, May, 1960.

10 from 30,000 to 60,000 each, and 4 from 10,000 to 30,000 each. The city statistical bureau, anticipating the need for statistical services in these communes, had early secured the approval of the local party committee for a scheme of organization and personnel, and then developed the work around the committee's focal-point program. When the value of statistical work was thus demonstrated, its professional status was recognized; this led to a great improvement in staffing. Now, a planning committee was set up at each subsidiary commune, with full-time personnel in charge of planning and statistics. Full- and part-time workers were also installed in every industrial unit, whether operated by the primary-level commune, by the subsidiary commune, or by the production brigades. Since the statistical workers were transferred from other lines of undertaking, they at first had little appreciation of the importance of their work, resulting in failure to make reports, in late reports, or in erroneous reports. Only through various forms of "thought education" was their morale uplifted. As with the services for rural communes, several operational systems of statistical control were introduced, namely, regular schedules, primary records, permanent files of materials, and statistical figures. However, the scope of application of statistical control was yet rather limited. For example, regular returns were required only of industrial and agricultural production; statistics for servicing stations, mess halls, and educational and cultural units were derived from irregular surveys. The primary record system had been installed thus far only for industrial-value product, industrial physical product, the industrial working force, industrial wages, and agricultural output.

It must be kept in mind that Chengchow has gone far beyond most other cities in communization. It has been reported that only the cities in Honan, Hopei, and Heilungkiang provinces were organized into communes by the end of

1959. Although an upsurge of the movement in other provinces took place in 1960, there is no doubt that a long distance remains before statistical services are in a position to cover adequately the "small indigenous and nonindigenous groups" of worksheds and workshops.

# CHAPTER XIII

# Summary and Evaluation

This study posed the problem of evaluating the validity of Chinese statistics through an investigation of the development of its statistical system. The development up to 1957 was evaluated in chapter vi; it remains to bring this evaluation up to 1960.

Since starting operation in October, 1952, the State Bureau had been dedicated to establishing a state statistical system with centralized control over all technical matters relating to the compilation of national statistics, including collection, computation, and publication. The end of the first five-year-plan period saw the extension of the services to industrial centers and large-sized centrally controlled economic enterprises. The bureau was unable to operate much beyond the special-district level, failing to set up regular working offices at the strategic *hsien* level despite three years of effort from 1955 through 1957. During the period of the second five-year plan, the bureau set forth as its major task the extension of the services all the way to the villages and agricultural collectives, as well as improvement of the keeping of primary records in enterprises.

In 1958, however, the decentralization program and the great-leap movement brought new responsibility and authority to the party committees of various local levels. Each of these committees claimed and exercised operational as well as jurisdictional control over the local statistical offices, if only for the sake of preparing background statistics, comparative statistics, and, above all, progress statistics in relation to the party committee's focal-point programs. The principle of complete enumeration embodied in the regular statistical schedules was condemned in favor of the method of model survey that admirably served the purpose of progress statistics. With reluctance the bureau yielded to this strong pressure during the national statistical work reform movement of the third quarter of 1958, in which the policy of mass participation in statistical work under local party leadership had orginated. In the meantime, the reform movement of rural statistical work was already in progress, resulting in the establishment of services at the *hsien, hsiang,* and agricultural-collective levels, operated by local party secretaries to the exclusion of the State Bureau's influence. At the provincial and city levels local party leadership also came to dominate the services through virtually taking over management of all economic enterprises of any importance and dictating the role of the state statistical offices concerned. Even in the central government the State Bureau was fast reduced to playing a passive, secondary role by the business-affairs ministries: it was the Ministry of Agriculture which issued statistical communiqués on "great leaps" in farm output during the summer and autumn harvests of the year. Moreover, the policy of mass participation under local party leadership soon led the local party and government authorities to deny the professional and scientific nature of statistical work, and to question the need for a national network of state statistical offices and even for separate statistical units in business-affairs departments and enterprises. Toward the end of the year many of these statistical units were discontinued. Thus it is not far from the truth that in 1958 the whole state statistical system was being scraped, to be replaced by a completely decentralized, highly fragmented, local-party-committee-directed, nonspecialized operation, engaged mostly in the compilation of progress statistics for local focal-point programs.

The statistical fiasco of 1958 vindicated the State Bureau and its unified operational policy as much as it convinced the central party authorities of the necessity to uphold the integrity of the state statistical system. Probably, the growing problems of holding local party committees in line with the policies of the center also helped. At any rate the system emerged from the 1958 experience with a national organization much more penetrating and far more effective than the bureau had ever anticipated.

In 1959 statistical services were restored and strengthened in state enterprises at the insistence of the city statistical bureaus. Services began to be installed in many urban communes established in the industrial and mining centers. In the rural areas the bureau was brought back to the scene, charged with the responsibility of conducting farm-output surveys and of organizing "accurate statistical services" in rural communes. The huge working force required was recruited from among the cadres who had a relatively high degree of political understanding, a strong sense of responsibility, good relations with the masses, and an elementary ability for computation. Their training, for which the state system was responsible, centered on the basic knowledge of processing regular statistical schedules. The organizational drive was pushed hard enough in 1960 to warrant the bureau to make a national check during the year on the progress made. For both urban and rural areas, mass participation was still stressed, but in essence it meant the mobilization of production workers on the job to undertake the keeping of primary records in enterprises and of original records in communes.

Another momentous change was the integration of the statistical services of the business-affairs ministries and departments into the state system in 1959. Each local office of the system was given the highest operational authority in statistical matters at that particular level of government. In some provinces, and perhaps in others as well, the business-affairs departments and other government agencies were directed to see to it that all important comprehensive figures, whether for publication, internal use, or reporting to higher authorities, had to be consistent with those prepared by the local statistical office on the same level. In the central government the Ministry of Agriculture no longer issued statistical communiqués. The unified nature of statistical work was widely recognized.

Thus, in 1959 and 1960 the state statistical system had made a great advance in organization. For the first time since its establishment in 1952 the State Bureau was more or less in a position to maintain a direct line of operational command all the way down to the primary levels in the communes, state enterprises, and business-affairs departments. How have all these developments affected the quality of statistics?

There is no reason to modify what has been said in chapter vi about the relative strength of the foundations for the different types of functional statistics as of the end of 1957. In 1958, a general deterioration occurred in all fields, with the extent of deterioration being an inverse function of the relative strength of its foundation. Since then, the change in the quality of national statistics has been closely related to the developments in the four areas of progress statistics, agricultural statistics, model surveys, and the partisanship principle.

The recovery and expansion of the state statistical system since 1958 would not have been possible without the active support and leadership of the local party committees. In view of what happened in 1958, such support was forthcoming only at a price—the supply of statistical data to these committees for their focal-point programs. These programs are generally concerned with emulative drives, preliminary and final distri-

bution of "income" among commune members, allocation of
tax and state-purchase quotas, and checking on the production
and marketing plans; all of them require progress statistics
for the purpose of planning, checking, and publicizing. From
the standpoint of the state service the wide application of
progress statistics has the merit of educating local authorities
and the public to the importance of statistics, keeping the
rank and file fully occupied throughout the year, and, therefore, enlisting the active support of local party secretaries.

All progress statistics, however, are upward-biased. As
Hsüeh revealed on the eve of his departure from the State
Bureau, timeliness is much more important than accuracy for
some types of statistics, which, therefore, should not be taken
at their face value. Progress statistics belong to this category.
But the problem goes deeper than this significant admission
indicates. For, in many instances, pure falsification of data
have been discovered. And the extent of it depends on the
pressure to reach a target. The continuous upward revision
of output targets, with failures attributed only to the serious
errors of rightist conservatism, is the most important single
reason for the statistical debacle of 1958.

Since 1958, however, the pressure has been very much
eased. Accuracy in statistics was introduced as a national
slogan early in 1959. More important was the fact that despite
the antirightist campaign, Premier Chou, in his famous August,
1959 statement, admitted that the government had fallen into
the error of setting the output goals too high for 1959 and that
the revised targets for the year represented a "leap" rather
than a "great leap." The experience with the agricultural
"eight-word charter" also brought home the lesson that its
rigid application had wrought more harm than good and that
considerable allowance should be made for local experimentation and adjustment without counting on an immediate substantial increase in output. Finally, the practice of continuous

upward revision of output targets has ceased. It is not clear whether the method of "planning with two accounts" was still operative in 1959, but no more mention of it has been found since 1958 in the joint official journal of the State Bureau and the State Planning Commission. Thus the cadres have not been subject to the same pressure to pad their statistics as they were in 1958. Nevertheless, under all circumstances, progress statistics, for which timeliness is more important than accuracy, must be set apart from the annual finalized figures derived from the statistical returns.

Agricultural statistics were as much the "weakest link" in the statistical front in 1961 as they were in 1957. The 1958 debacle affected agricultural statistics much more seriously than industrial or other statistics, because of the lack of statistical controls over reporting from the countryside. No original records were kept of output, and model surveys were used to produce any desirable results. *Ex post* checking on output data, particularly after the lapse of a winter and a spring, serves no purpose, because consumption, among other data, could not be retraced. The amount of grains that have been both collected for taxes and purchased by the state constitutes the only tangible evidence; but the tax rates and the purchase quotas are determined as ratios to estimated output—ratios that may turn out to be too high in terms of actual output as they must have been in 1958. In other words, to reëstimate the 1958 output on the basis of tax collection and state purchases, as was done in the late spring of 1959, tended to overstate output, unless the central party authorities were prepared to admit that the amount that went into the hands of the state bore an exceptionally high proportion to output. As the national conference of provincial bureau directors concluded, "output investigations cannot be separated from the actual process of crop growth." This certainly explains why, even after a national check on an unprecedented scale, the

State Bureau has remained unsatisfied with the final, heavily scaled-down figures for the agricultural output of 1958. For reasons just stated, these figures must still exaggerate substantially the agricultural output of the year.

Since 1958 serious effort has been made to improve agricultural statistics. Farm-output investigations on a national scale, started in 1959, have been an important development. Local committees have been organized all over the countryside by state statistical officers under the leadership of local party secretaries to survey summer and autumn harvests. A survey usually begins with a visual estimate of output at the time of crop growth, and proceeds with choice of stratified model areas, then sample cutting during harvest, and, finally, computation of the harvest. Up to 1959 the computed output was to be checked against the actual biological yield; but since then, the barn yield has been officially adopted as the measure of output. While these output investigations, long advocated by the State Bureau, represent a big step forward, two problems have emerged with regard to statistics: First, that it will take an indeterminate amount of time before all localities and provinces effectively and uniformly adopt the practice of reckoning output in terms of barn yield; in the meantime there is bound to be confusion, which will affect the quality of provincial or national aggregates. Second, comparability between the figures of the 1950's and those of the 1960's—a problem that can be solved only by personal judgment.

The development of rural statistical services should in due time contribute more information on the rural economy. For the present, however, rural statistics still center on agricultural statistics, with increasing attention given to industrial and transportation statistics. Statistical control systems—original records, permanent files, and unified schedules and figures —have begun to be introduced into the rural area. It is, of course, too early to tell how they will work out in practice, but there is no denying that they are genuine innovations meeting the real needs of the situation. The huge statistical working force, full-time, part-time, and on-the-job, will take some time to acquire the skill of handling the schedules, but the fact that the beginning has been made is important to the quality of rural statistics.

In contrast to its policy up to 1957, the State Bureau has become reconciled to the fact that the method of model survey is destined to play a vital role for a long time in the statistics of agriculture and of small indigenous and nonindigenous groups of enterprises. It is the simplest method for compiling all those statistics that require timeliness rather than accuracy. It is the earliest for the rank-and-file to learn and for local party secretaries to understand. However, as it has been used, the method is hardly a statistical tool. Now, control over its application is being introduced. The State Bureau has insisted that model surveys may be used as a check against the comprehensive statistical returns, but not as a substitute for them. Moreover, the statistical offices at the *hsien* level are each required to conduct by themselves as many of the statistical surveys requested from them as possible, instead of passing them on to the lower and less competent levels. In 1960, above all, a number of "typical" *hsien,* communes, and production teams were chosen from each province to serve as fixed reporting units for all stratified model surveys; they receive direct technical aid from the bureau and maintain direct contact with it. As for the cities, the gradual organization of services in the urban communes would reduce the need for securing data from small-sized enterprises by model surveys. And in 1960, statistical services were introduced for the first time in small basic construction units and small nonindigenous enterprises.[1] Before these efforts

---

[1] Another "first" in 1960 was statistical service for technological improvement and innovation. For definition of "small basic construction unit," see my *Economic Development of Communist China,* p. 11 n.

bear fruit, however, the quality of all functional statistics, because of the mushroom growth of small-sized enterprises since 1957, will continue to vary inversely with the importance of the "small-sized" component—unless, in the meantime, the bureau is authorized to release statistics that would sharply differentiate not only the nonindigenous from the indigenous, but under each category also the large from the medium and the small.

Having weathered the tremendous onslaught in 1958, the five guiding principles of the state statistical service have remained on the whole intact, with one great modification. Whereas statistics were taken as the servant of national planning, they must now serve politics, production, the masses, the leadership, and planning—in that order. This is a concise statement of the partisanship principle in statistics, with which the national conference of provincial and city bureau directors in October, 1959, was exclusively concerned. Under the principle, statistics must reflect nothing but achievements. If the data collected point up failures or troubles, they must be reported only to the proper authorities, lest the rightist elements in the party and government machinery use them to criticize or discredit the central party leadership. The implication is that statistical workers are well advised not to collect, much less to make public, materials damaging to the present central authorities. Thus, instead of being essentially a technical tool for planning, statistics have begun taking on the character of a political weapon for intraparty strife, as they once were so regarded in the 1930's.

The partisanship principle also stresses more than ever the prerogative of local party leadership to review and finalize all comprehensive statistical figures. Thus, resurgence of the state statistical system after the 1958 disaster does not imply any immediate improvement in the validity of official statistics, particularly in agriculture. The fact that statistical services

have come to be dominated by local party committees is sufficient to cast doubt on the accuracy of statistical reporting.
The considerations of the local leaders may be political in
nature, or based on results derived from independent model
surveys or other sources. There is evidence that the state
statistical hierarchy has tended to insist on the accuracy of its
own figures which may be different from those reviewed and
finalized by local party and government authorities. It has
been reported that in many a commune two or three different
sets of figures were prepared, representing the divergent
results from progress statistics, regular returns, and model
surveys. Efforts are being made in the communes to unify
the figures. On the national level important figures have to be
finalized by the State Council at the recommendation of the
State Bureau. Since the bureau generally has a much stronger
voice than local party authorities in the State Council, the
factor of such bias as comes from local review should probably
be less important in national statistics than in provincial or
other local statistics.

The future will reveal how far the state statistical service
would and could assert itself in improving national statistics.
In the meanwhile, we may be sure that statistics are released
primarily to serve the purposes and objectives of the Chinese
Communist party. However, if it is true that only statistics
of achievements are published while those reflecting difficulties
and problems are either withheld or not collected at all, then
there are not likely to be two sets of national statistics, one
for planning and the other for propaganda. Furthermore, we
may be equally sure that with this one set of figures even
the State Statistical Bureau has been far from satisfied with
its truthfulness. For the purpose of economic analysis, adjustment of the different component series will doubtless be a
subject challenging to our imagination and ingenuity for a
long time.

# Bibliography

I. CHINESE-LANGUAGE SOURCES:

A. Books:

Directorate General of Budgets, Accounts and Statistics, Bureau of Statistics. *Chung-hua-min-kuo t'ung-chi nien-chien* [Statistical Yearbook of the Republic of China]. Nanking: June, 1948.

Ministry of Agriculture, Bureau of Planning. *Chung-kuo yü shih-chieh chu-yao kuo-chia nung-yeh sheng-chan t'ung-chi tzu-liao hui-p'ien* [Compendium of the Agricultural Production Statistics of China and other Major Countries of the World]. Peiping: October, 1958.

State Statistical Bureau. *Nung-yeh t'ung-chi kung-tso shou-tse* [Handbook for Agricultural Statistical Work]. Peiping: June, 1956.

————. *Wei-ta ti shih-nien* [The Great Ten Years]. Peiping: September, 1959.

B. Communiqués:

1. Chinese Communist Party, Central Committee:
   "Communiqué of the Eighth Plenary Session," *JMJP*, August 27, 1959.
   "Communiqué of the Ninth Plenary Session," *JMJP*, January 21, 1961.
   "Communiqué of the Sixth Plenary Session on the National Economic Plan of 1959," *JMJP*, December 18, 1958.

2. Ministry of Agriculture:
   "Communiqué on the 1958 Output of Early Rice," *JMJP*, October 13, 1958.
   "Communiqué on the 1958 Output of Rapeseed," *JMJP*, October 13, 1958.
   "Communiqué on the 1958 Output of Spring Wheat," *JMJP*, October 13, 1958.

"Communiqué on the 1958 Output of Summer-harvested Food Grains," *JMJP*, July 23, 1958.
3. State Statistical Bureau:
"Communiqué on Correction of the 1958 Agricultural Statistics," *JMJP*, August 27, 1959.
"Communiqué on the Fulfillment of the First Five-Year Plan," *JMJP*, April 14, 1959.
"Communiqué on the Results of the 1958 Plan," *JMJP*, April 15, 1959.
C. EDITORIALS:
"Celebrate our Great National Anniversary," *JMJP*, October 1, 1960.
"Depend on the Masses for Setting up Statistical Network in the *Hsien, Hsiang,* and Agricultural Collectives," *JMJP*, April 29, 1958.
"Develop the Practice of Verification," *CHYTC*, 2 (January, 1959), 1–2.
"The National Statistical Work Reform is Basically Completed," *TCKT*, 19 (October, 1958), 6–8.
"The Necessity of Bringing about an All-Front Leap in Rural Statistical Work," *CHYTC*, 2 (February, 1960), 4–6.
"The Need to Perform Statistical Services Diligently, Fast, Well, and Economically in Order to Meet National Construction Needs," *TCKTTH*, 2 (January, 1956), 3–6.
"Raise the Level of Statistical work from the Present Base!" *TCKTTH*, 1 (January, 1955), 1–4.
"Statistical Services also Require Technological Innovation by the Masses," *CHYTC*, 2 (February, 1960), 30–31.
"Statistical Work must Meet the Needs of National Construction," *JMJP*, February 22, 1956.
"Strengthen the Control over Statistical Schedules and Overcome the Present Situation of Too Many Schedules," *CHYTC*, 9 (June, 1959), 1–2.
"Strengthen the Training and Education of Statistical Workers," *TCKTTH*, 2 (May, 1954), 1–2.
"Strive to Meet the Major Targets of the Second Five-Year Plan in the Current Year," *JMJP*, August 27, 1959.
"To Further Strengthen Statistical Work in the Period of Economic Construction," *JMJP*, March 31, 1954.

"To Our Readers and Authors," *TCKT*, 1 (January, 1957), 3–4.

" 'The Whole Country as a Game of Chess' is the Basic Assurance to Realize the 1959 Leap-Forward Plan," *CHYTC*, 4 (February, 1959), 1–2.

D. Signed Articles, Statements, and Directives:

Anhwei Province, Planning Commission. "Preliminary Evaluation of Surveys of Agricultural Output of 1959 in Anhwei Province," *CHYTC*, 2 (February, 1960), 22–26.

Ch'ai Mou. "The Superiority of People's Communes from the Viewpoint of Fiscal and Trading Work," *CCYC*, 11 (November, 1959), 34–37 and 65.

Chang Cheng. "Several Problems of Sampling in Agricultural-Output Surveys," *TCYC*, 4 (April, 1958), 27–31.

Chang Lin-chih. "Strive for a High Growth Rate in the Coal Industry," *JMJP*, October 7, 1959.

Chang Mu-yao. "Statement at the National Conference," *JMJP*, April 14, 1960.

Chao I-wen. "My Recognition of Dogmatism in Statistical Services," *TCYC*, 5 (May, 1958), 9–12.

Chen Ying-chung. "A Wider Application of the Method of Model Survey," *CHYTC*, 6 (March, 1959), 34–36.

Ch'eng Chen-chia. "A Great Leap in Planning under the Anti-Waste and Anti-Conservatism Movement," *CHCC*, 4 (April, 1958), 5–6.

Cheng Ching-ch'ing. "The Great Achievements of China's Socialist Construction in the Past Ten Years," *CCYC*, 10 (October, 1959), 1–10.

Chi Chung-wei. "China's Industry Must Positively Assist and Promote the Development of Agriculture," *CCYC*, 2 (February, 1958), 1–11.

Chia Ch'i-yun. "Conclusions from the Discussion on 'Why Unwilling to Engage in Statistical Work?' " *TCKTTH*, 12 (December, 1955), 7–11.

————. "Excerpt of the Speech at the National Conference of Directors of Provincial and City Statistical Bureaus," *CHYTC*, 14 (November, 1959), 1–5.

————. "Final Evaluation of Statistical Work at the National Conference of Directors of Provincial and City Statistical Bureaus," *CHYTC*, 14 (November, 1959), 6–8.

————. "On the Problems of Policy concerning China's Statistical Work," *CHYTC*, 10 (July, 1959), 1–6.

————. "Report at the Fourth National Statistical Conference," *TCKTTH*, 3 (March, 1955), 1–9.

————. "Several Problems in the Present Reform Movement of Statistical Services," *TCKT*, 15 (August, 1958), 5–10.

————. "Study Conscientiously the Resolutions of the Party's Central Committee and Raise the Ideological Level of Statistical Workers," *TCKTTH*, 2 (May, 1954), 3–6.

Chia Fu. "On the Growth Rate of the National Economy during the Period of the Second Five-Year Plan," *CHCC*, 10 (October, 1956), 4–7.

Chiang Chao. "What are Statistics and Their Functions?" *TCKTTH*, 2 (May, 1954), 27–31.

Chou En-lai. "Report on Revision of the Major Targets in the 1959 Plan and on Stepping up the Movement for Increasing Output and Economizing," *JMJP*, August 29, 1959.

————. "Report on the Work of the Government," *JMJP*, April 19, 1959.

Chuang Chung. "Evaluation of the Experience from Strengthening Partisanship in Statistical Services, and Raising the Theoretical Level of China's Statistics," *CHYTC*, 2 (February, 1960), 35 and 21.

Hsia Szu-p'ing. "Statistical Work in Recent Years as Viewed from Planning," *TCKT*, 17 (September, 1957), 17–18.

Hsu Chien. "To Service Planning is the Basic Duty of Statistical Work," *TCKTTH*, 1 (April, 1954), 17–19.

Hsüeh Mu-ch'iao. "Director Hsüeh's Concluding Report at the National Statistical Conference at Paoting," *TCKT*, 14 (July, 1958), 2–8.

————. "Director Hsüeh's Report at the Sixth National Statistical Conference," *TCKT*, 21 (November, 1957), 1–21.

————. "Director Hsüeh's Report at the Third National Statistical Conference," *TCKTTH*, 1 (April, 1954), 4–11.

————. "Final Report at the Fourth National Statistical Conference," *TCKTTH*, 5 (May, 1955), 1–7.

————. "How does Statistical Work Make a Great Leap?" *TCKT*, 5 (March, 1958), 1–5.

————. "Record of Director Hsüeh's Report at the Meeting of All Bureau Workers," *TCKT*, 6 (March, 1957), 1–6.

————. "Record of Director Hsüeh's Remarks at the Statistical Meeting in Honan Province," *TCKT*, 12 (June, 1958), 1–4.

————. "Report at the National Meeting on Agricultural Statistical Work," *TCKT*, 22 (November, 1957), 7–11.

————. "Several Important Questions in Statistical Theory," *CHYTC*, 8 (May, 1959), 5–9.

————. "Statistical Workers Must Rise to Struggle against the Rightists," *TCKT*, 16 (August, 1957), 1–4.

————. "To Establish a Unified Control System of Agricultural Statistical Service is the Road to Develop Statistical Work in the *Hsien*," *TCKT*, 8 (April, 1958), 1–4.

Hsüeh Yi-yuen. "The Division of Administrative Areas of the People's Republic of China," *Ti-li hsüeh-pao* [Journal of Geography], 24 (February, 1958), 84–97.

Hu Kai-ming. "Remarks at the National Statistical Meeting (Paoting, Hopei)," *TCKT*, 13 (June, 1958), 3–6.

Huang Chien-t'o. "Chief Tasks in the Agricultural Statistical Work Program for 1960," *CHYTC*, 2 (February, 1960), 18–21.

————. "Exert Effort to Improve Agricultural Statistical Services," *TCKT*, 8 (April, 1957), 5–8.

Huang Hai. "Several Problems of Regular Industrial Statistical Schedules," *TCKTTH*, 1 (April, 1954), 23–27.

Hunan Province, Changsha *Hsien*, Kao-tang People's Commune, Party Committee. "Establish Proper Statistical Organization for People's Communes," *TCKT*, 18 (September, 1958), 25–26.

Hunan Province, Hua-yung *Hsien*, Planning Committee. "Draft Regulations concerning the Organization of Planning-Statistical Committees in People's Communes," *TCKT*, 18 (September, 1958), 26.

Hupei Province, Ngo-ch'eng *Hsien*, Planning Committee. "How the Planning Committee of Hsü-kwong People's

Commune Develops Planning and Statistical Work," *CHCC*, 10 (October, 1958), 17–18.

Kung Chang-chen. "The Present Tasks in Transportation Statistics," *CHYTC*, 11 (August, 1959), 4–5.

Kuo Yung-hua. "The Establishment and Development of Statistical Services in the Urban Communes of Chengchow," *CHYTC*, 5 (May, 1960), 20–21.

Li Chi-p'ing. "How has the Party Directed and Utilized Statistical Services?" *TCKT*, 13 (July, 1958), 7–13.

Li Chu-ch'en. "Foster a Great Leap in China's Food Industry," *HHPYK*, 7 (April, 1958), 51–53.

———. "Report at the People's Congress," *JMJP*, July 12, 1957.

Li Fei-tang. "A New Phase of Rural Statistical Work," *CHYTC*, 5 (May, 1960), 9–10 and 36.

Li Fu-ch'un. "Report on the Draft Plan for 1959," *JMJP*, April 22, 1959.

———. "Report on the Draft Plan for 1960," *JMJP*, March 31, 1960.

Li Hsieh-po. "The Working Class and Urban Communes," *JMJP*, April 9, 1960.

Li Hsien-nien. "Report on the Realized Budget of 1957 and on the Planned Budget for 1958," *HHPYK*, 5 (March, 1958), 4.

Li Kuang-yin. "Ten-Year Achievements in China's Health Statistics," *Jen-min pao-chien* [People's Health], 10 (October, 1959), 923–926.

Li P'ing-heng. "Unlimited Advantages of Organized Living," *JMJP*, April 9, 1960.

Liao Chi-li. "About the Two-Account System," *CHCC*, 5 (May, 1958), 8–9.

Liao Lu-yen. "Final Evaluation of the 1956 Operations in Agricultural Production and Major Tasks for 1957," *HHPYK*, 8 (April, 1957), 81–88.

———. "Tasks at the 1959 Agricultural Battle Front," *HC*, 1 (January, 1959), 11–18.

Liu Shao-ch'i. "The Triumph of Marxism-Leninism in China," *JMJP*, October 1, 1959.

Ma Heng-chih. "How to Investigate the Quality of Statistical Figures in Factories and Mines," *TCKTTH*, 3 (March, 1955), 10–14.

Ministry of Agriculture, Bureau of Food Crop Production. "Food Production during the period of the First Five-Year Plan," *HHPYK*, 9 (May, 1958), 80–83.

Ministry of the Textile Industry, Dairen Spinning and Weaving Mill. "How has my Mill Eliminated Fictitious Figures on Output and Efficiency," *TCKTTH*, 7 (October, 1954), 31–33.

Mo Yueh-ta, Chu Hung-en and T'ung Cheng-hui. "The So-called Statistical Legacy from Old China and the Processing of These Materials in Recent Years," *TCKT*, 16 (August, 1957), 24–27 and 14.

Ou Ming. "On the Whole Country as a Game of Chess," *CHYTC*, 2 (January, 1959), 3–4.

Po I-po. "Report on the Draft Plan for 1958," *HHPYK*, 5 (March, 1958), 12–23.

————. "Report on the Results of the 1956 Plan and on the Plan for 1957," *JMJP*, July 2, 1957.

————. "Strive for new Triumphs in the Development of China's Industrial Production," *HC*, 3–4 (February, 1961), 19–25.

————. "The Tasks at the 1959 Industrial Front," *HC*, 1 (January, 1959), 6–10.

State Planning Commission. "Unified Regulations concerning Some Problems in Planning and Statistical Work," *TCKTTH*, 7 (October, 1954), 11–12.

State Statistical Bureau. "A Directive on Specialized Statistical Training of on-the-job Workers," *TCKTTH*, 5 (May, 1955), 8–9.

————. "A Directive concerning the Development of Analytical Work on Industrial Statistics," *TCKTTH*, 6 (September, 1954), 4–6.

————. "A Directive concerning the Strengthening of Industrial Statistical Work," *TCKTTH*, 6 (September, 1954), 1–3.

————. "Some Provisions concerning the Relationship in Statistical Work between Provincial and City Statistical Bureaus and Those of State-operated Enterprises and

Construction Units," *TCKTTH*, 7 (October, 1954), 13–14.

——. "National Program for Statistical Work, 1956–1957," *TCKTTH*, 11 (June, 1956), 1–3.

——. "Replies to Some Questions," *TCKTTH*, 4 (July, 1954), 41–43.

——. Department of Agricultural Statistics. "The Program of Agricultural Statistical Work for 1955," *TCKTTH*, 1 (January, 1955), 8–11.

——, Department of Education. "Some Problems of Improving the Statistical Training Courses," *TCKT*, 3 (February, 1957), 26–27.

——, Department of Industrial Statistics. "Basic Conclusions from Reviewing the Work on National Industrial Statistics of 1954 and the Work Program for 1955," *TCKTTH*, 9 (December, 1954), 1–7.

——, Office of Statistical Materials. "The Basic Condition of China's Coal Industry," *TCYC*, 4 (April, 1958), 18–23.

——, Office of Statistical Materials. "The Situation of China's Light Industry," *TCYC*, 2 (February, 1958), 12–15.

——, Department of Trade Statistics. "Explanations of some Problems concerning the Unified Catalogue of Commodities in Internal Trade," *TCKTTH*, 9 (December, 1954), 38–41.

Szechwan Provincial Statistical Bureau. "Basic Evaluation of the Work in Establishing Accurate Statistical Services in People's Communes in Szechwan Province," *CHYTC*, 2 (February, 1960), 26–29.

T'ao Yen. "Report at the Wuhan Meeting of Statistical Workers," *TCYC*, 5 (May, 1958), 4–8.

Teng Chung-yi. "Basic Experience from Organizing City Statistical Services for an All-Front Great Leap," *CHYTC*, 5 (May, 1960), 15–19.

Teng I-chuan. "Excerpt of Teng's Remarks at the Joint Meeting of Party Secretaries and Statistical-Unit Chiefs of the *Hsien* Level," *TCKT*, 12 (June, 1958), 5–8.

Ti Ch'ao-po. "Exert Effort to Complete the National Industrial Survey," *JMJP*, April 10, 1950.

Ti Ching-hsiang. "Increase Sugar Output for the People," *TKP*, January 5, 1958.

Tien Ch'i. "The Double-tracked System," *TCKTTH*, 5 (May, 1956), 41.

Tung Shao-hua. "Our Work in Taking Care of Statistical Materials," *TCKTTH*, 19 (October, 1956), 31–33.

Wang I-fu. "On the Problem of Improving the System of Industrial Statistical Returns," *TCYC*, 7 (July, 1958), 9–13.

————. "Struggle for Improving the Accuracy of Industrial Statistical Figures," *TCKTTH*, 3 (March, 1955), 15–17.

Wang Keng-chin. "Some Points of my Understanding of Agricultural Planning," *CHYTC*, 14 (November, 1959), 15–21.

Wang Kwong-wei. "The Tasks of the State Planning Commission," *CHCC*, 2 (February, 1956), 11–14.

Wang Szu-hua. "On a Great Contradiction in China's Statistical Work at the Present," *TCKT*, 15 (August, 1957), 8–11.

————. "The Problem of Relative Importance between Industrial and Agricultural Production in the Northeast," *JMJP*, November 3, 1949.

Wei Heng. "Develop the Practice of Verification and Establish Accurate Statistical Services," *CHYTC*, 6 (March, 1959), 1–3.

Wei I. "Revolution in the Method of Planning," *HH*, 8 (April, 1958), 10–12.

Wu Kwong-t'ang. "Experience in Agricultural-Output Surveys," *CHYTC*, 11 (August, 1959), 6–7.

Wu Po, "Explanations for the Draft Regulations of Agricultural Tax of the People's Republic of China," *JMJP*, June 5, 1958.

Yang Chien-pao. "Exert Effort to Develop further the Work on Comprehensive Statistics," *TCKTTH*, 5 (May, 1955), 10–13.

————. "On the Proportionate Relationship as the Basic Nature of a National Economy," *CCYC*, 10 (October, 1959), 11–25.

Yang Po. "Has the Direction of our Statistical Work been Wrong?" *TCKT*, 16 (August, 1957), 10–14.

————. "How to Conduct Model Surveys," *CHYTC*, 1 (January, 1959), 36–37; 2 (January, 1959), 36–37; 3 (February, 1959), 24–25; 4 (February, 1959), 40–41; and 5 (March, 1959), 36–37.

Yang Ying-chieh. "The Principle of Balance in Planning for the National Economy," *HH*, 12 (June, 1958), 26–27.

Yen Shou-chih. "The Correctness of our Statistical Program Permits of no Criticism," *TCKT*, 16 (August, 1957), 22–23.

Yuen Po. "On the Direction of Statistical Work," *TCYC*, 7 (July, 1958), 5–8.

E. UNSIGNED ARTICLES, STATEMENTS, AND DISPATCHES:

"Administrative Divisions of China," in *1953 Jen-min shou-tse* [People's Handbook of 1953], Tientsin: 1954, 128–148.

"An Account of the National Conference of Provincial Statistical Bureau Directors," *TCKT*, 21 (November, 1958), 1–3.

"The Great Leap Forward," *Ts'ai-ching yen-chiu* [Financial and Economic Research], 3 (June, 1958), 5.

"The Gross Industrial Value Product of China for 1957," *Chin-jih hsin-wen* [Today's News], December 31, 1957.

"Joint Panel Discussion between the State Statistical Bureau and the Ministry of Agriculture on the Method of Surveying Crops Harvested," *TCKT*, 17 (September, 1957), 27.

"The National Conference on Statistical Work," *JMJP*, December 29, 1952.

"People's Communes are Good," *JMJP*, January 4, 1959.

"Report on the National Conference on Output Surveys of Summer Harvests," *CHYTC*, 11 (August, 1959), 8.

"Report on the National Meeting of Directors of Provincial Statistical Bureaus," *CHYTC*, 8 (May, 1959), 1–4.

"Statistical Services in the Rural Communes are being Initiated," *CHYTC*, 2 (January, 1959), 20.

"Strengthen Further the Statistical Work on Iron and Steel," *CHYTC*, 1 (January, 1959), 13–15.

"Training Course for the Statistical Workers of People's Communes in Chekiang Province," *CHYTC*, 2 (February, 1960), 9.

"Virtually all Agricultural Villages in China have been Communized," *TCKT*, 20 (October, 1958), 23.

II. ENGLISH-LANGUAGE AND
RUSSIAN-LANGUAGE SOURCES:

Government of India, Ministry of Food and Agriculture. *Report of Indian Delegation to China on Agricultural Planning and Techniques*. New Delhi: Government of India Press, 1956.

Grossman, Gregory. *Soviet Statistics of Physical Output of Industrial Commodities*. New Jersey: Princeton University Press, 1960.

Hsüeh, Mu-ch'iao. "Statistical Work in the People's Republic of China," *Vestnik Statistiki* [Statistical Herald], 7 (July, 1958), 20–24.

Li, Choh-Ming. "Economic Development," *The China Quarterly*, 1 (January-March, 1960), 35–50. Reprinted, with some revision, in Adamantios Pepelasis, Leon Mears, and Irma Adelman, *Economic Development: Analysis and Case Studies*, New York: Harpers and Brothers, 1961, 366–383.

———. *Economic Development of Communist China: An Appraisal of the First Five Years of Industrialization*. Berkeley and Los Angeles: University of California Press, 1959.

United States Consulate General, Hong Kong. *Current Background* (mimeographed), no. 434, January 15, 1957. Translation of the full text of *Nung-yeh t'ung-chi kung-tso shou-tse* [Handbook for Agricultural Statistical Work], Peiping, 1956.

# Indexes

# Subject Index

# Name Index